Praise for
Celebrate Marketing

"*Celebrate Marketing* is more than a good and useful book. It's just great! It can truly enrich your business and your life. And it will."
— Joe Batten, *Tough-Minded Leadership* and
The Master Motivator

"Superb! *Celebrate Marketing* is a truly practical guide on marketing. Its many marketing tools, tips, and techniques are clearly presented and, best of all, are highly entertaining and informative. Any person seriously interested in marketing will benefit from this book."
— Michael Michalko,
Thinkertoys: A Handbook and Business Creativity and
Cracking Creativity: The Secrets of Creative Genius

"Another winner! Getting and keeping customers is the #1 challenge for any business of any size. This wonderful book clearly shows you the secrets behind how to make it happen for your business."
—Bill Brooks, *Niche Selling*

"A virtual who's who of marketing experts tells you exactly what's what on dozens of ways to grow your business. Here's everything you need to successfully market your product or service."
— Richard F. Gerson, PhD,
Marketing Strategies for Small Businesses

"Effective, underused, and innovative marketing ideas not typically covered in books of this kind. Valuable."
— Bob Bly, *Selling Your Services*

"What a gem! Read it for marketing knowledge. Browse for ideas you can apply immediately."
— Jerry Michaelson, *Winning the Marketing War*

"You'll celebrate the day you buy this book—it's chock full of inspiring, personal lessons that almost any business can put to work right away. Every page seems to offer something new or gives a new twist to the tried and true."
— Richard Cross, *Customer Bonding*

"What I like best about *Celebrate Marketing* is that it's not just theory like so many marketing books. This book is packed with ideas that can produce results immediately. It's a must-read for any business owner or marketing director."
— Bill Cates, president, Referral Coaching International,
author, *Unlimited Referrals*

"Packed with tried-and-true marketing strategies from seasoned pros."
— Ron Willingham,
Integrity Selling

"Wow! An advanced course on marketing in lively, easy-to-implement chunks! Use its tips whenever you feel the urge to increase profits for your business. Don't read this book without a highlighter pen,"
— Marcia Yudkin,
Six Steps to Free Publicity

"*Celebrate Marketing* is *must* reading for everyone who is serious about getting and keeping customers. It is a treasury of good ideas."
— Jerry Wilson, *Word-of-Mouth Marketing*

"This book is right on the money."
— Lawrence W. Kohn, *Selling with Honor*

"*Celebrate Marketing* goes far beyond covering the typical four Ps of marketing. It provides many real-life examples of why some marketing strategies fail and why others can be right on target. I plan to incorporate the concepts I learned from this book in consulting with clients."
— Chuck Eason, director,
Napa Valley College Small Business Development Center

"*Celebrate Marketing* delivers proven and powerful positioning and marketing strategies for all businesses in any industry. Read this book thoroughly—apply each chapter's action steps and watch your business soar."
— Don L. Price,
Secrets of Personal Marketing Power

"Rick Crandall has done it again with this important addition to his popular series of marketing books. *Celebrate Marketing* is packed with valuable advice drawn from the best practices of successful business, large and small. It is readable, practical, and user friendly."
— Ronald E. Goldsmith, Ph.D.
Marketing Department,
Florida State University

"Great. I love the series format—it's so friendly and accessible. This book will be great to give to clients. It's loaded with smart ideas that can improve anyone's marketing."
— Salli Rasberry,
Marketing Without Advertising

Celebrate Marketing

Secrets of Success

Celebrate Marketing

Secrets of Success

Featuring chapters by:
Fred Berns • Noulan W. Bowker • Rick Crandall
Theodore W. Garrison III • Ray Leone
David Klaybor • James A. Ray • Donna Reeve
Jim Rhode • Ford Saeks • Sam Wieder

Edited by Rick Crandall

Sponsored by
The Institute for Effective Marketing

Select Press
Corte Madera, CA

Select Press
P.O. Box 37
Corte Madera, CA 94976-0037
(415) 435-4461
SelectPr@aol.com

Other books in this series:

Celebrate Selling the Consultative-Relationship Way (1998)
Celebrate Customer Service: Insider Secrets (1999)

Bulk sales/pricing available.

Celebrate Marketing: Secrets of Success/
Rick Crandall (editor)

ISBN 1-890777-07-2

Printed in the United States of America
10 9 8 7 6 5 4 3 2 1

Celebrate Marketing

DARE TO BE DIFFERENT
Super Positioning

Fred Berns

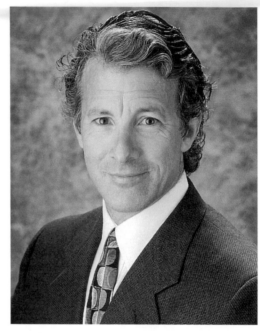

Fred Berns
is a consultant and speaker, and is author of sales and marketing books and tapes. His highly acclaimed presentations for corporations, associations, franchise organizations, and other groups focus on how individuals can use personal promotion to achieve peak sales performance. He has worked with organizations as diverse as Johnson & Johnson, the American Automobile Association, the American Society of Interior Designers, *Entrepreneur* magazine's Small Business Expos, the Environmental Protection Agency, and New York Life Insurance.

Mr. Berns also consults with organizations and individuals on how they can differentiate themselves, communicate more effectively, and make a maximum impact for a minimum investment of time and money.

His new book, *Sell Yourself! 501 Ways to Get Them to Buy from You*, became a national best-seller and led to the creation of "International Toot Your Flute Day," an event commemorated in *Chase's Calendar of Annual Events*.

Berns launched his speaking and consulting career after working in journalism for 25 years. He founded the Berns Bureau, and helped it become one of Washington DC's largest and longest-established independent news services.

Fred Berns, Power Promotion, 394 Rendezvous Dr., Lafayette, CO 80026; phone (303) 665-6688 or (888) 665-5505; fax (303) 665-5599; e-mail FredTalks@aol.com.

DARE TO BE DIFFERENT
Super Positioning

Fred Berns

In order to be irreplaceable one must always be
different.
—Coco Chanel

You are one of a kind. There never has been, nor
will there ever be another exactly like you.
Your "only" factor gives you a powerful uniqueness
you can use. Your marketing should reflect your
differences. These differences—your unique
strengths—can help others in unique ways.

THE POWER OF "ONLY"

I discovered the power of "only" months after
I set out to establish an independent radio news
service in Washington, DC, in 1976. My idea was
to provide localized news out of the nation's capital
for radio stations—news of specific interest to their
listeners.

I intended to report on the votes of local Congressmen, cover the testimony at Congressional hearings of visiting local city officials, and produce stories on hometown folks who had relocated in Washington. To personalize my telephone reports, I planned to sign them off with my name and the station's call letters.

Weeks on the road trying to sell radio news directors throughout the Midwest on the idea of my freelance service yielded few results. "Thanks, but no thanks" was the response I received from news directors from St. Louis to St. Paul.

Finally, two stations, KOLT in Scottsbluff, Nebraska, and KFIZ in Fond du Lac, Wisconsin, agreed to try out my service. The deal: $5 for every story of mine that they used on the air.

Advertising Doesn't Work

I was flush with the feeling of self-importance when I returned home to Washington. I was convinced that once I advertised the fact that I was in business, other radio station news directors would come running.

They didn't.

The costly ads I took out in various broadcasting trade publications yielded nothing. The longer I sat in my new office, the quieter it became. The calls didn't come in. My patience was running out. So was my money.

One morning I attended a workshop for new businesses conducted by the Small Business Administration's SCORE staff. The first speaker suggested that we "Look around at your neighbors, because two out of three of them will be out of business within 18 months." It wasn't exactly the motivational boost I was seeking!

The Only One of Its Kind

During a break I related my concerns about my business to a classmate. His suggestion: "package" the business differently, and refer to it in a press release to *Broadcasting Magazine* as the "only bureau of its kind with clients around the nation."

"'Clients around the nation?'" I replied. "You're saying I should promote that, even though I work only occasionally with one small station in Wisconsin and a smaller one in Nebraska?"

"Why not?" he replied. "What do you have to lose?"

A week later I wrote my first press release, a mere paragraph on my brand new letterhead stationery, announcing that I had launched the only independent news service of its kind serving radio stations "around the country." Within a few days after *Broadcasting Magazine* ran the blurb in its radio column, calls came in from news directors seeking more information about this "one of a kind" news service serving radio stations around the country.

The Only Bureau Of Its Kind With Clients Around The Nation!

Six weeks after the blurb appeared, 35 news directors had signed up to use the only service of its kind for stations "around the country."

Several months later, a radio station called from Toronto to ask for written transcripts for some Congressional hearing. After that, I started promoting my bureau as the only one of its kind serving stations "around the world." Inquiries came in from Australia, New Zealand, England, West Germany, Japan, and South Africa.

By the time I sold the Berns Bureau in April, 1992, it was the only news organization of its kind that over a 16-year period had served more than 5,000 broadcast and print outlets—around the country and around the world.

Basic Marketing: Find a Need

Developing your unique position starts with the basics. Your "basics" should begin with a personal message or commercial.

We tend to discuss our "features" ("I am very knowledgeable in the field of personal fitness training"). But our prospects are more interested in the benefits we can provide them ("I will help you improve your endurance and muscle tone").

For others to do as we want them to do—sign a contract, adopt a policy, grant a request for a raise or promotion—they need to perceive a personal benefit.

In the long run, the people you want to do business with don't care a great deal about your state-of-the-art technology, your hardware or your software. Nor are they necessarily persuaded by multimillion dollar advertising campaigns. Rather, they are motivated by what they think they will *get* by doing business with you. I will buy from you what you want to sell me *if* it will help my company make money, save money, or save time.

Your Target Group

As important as it is for us to spell out our unique benefits, it is vital that you target a unique audience. So often I ask sales professionals who their clients are. Far too often I get the response: "Anyone who will buy my products."

I don't know who "anyone" is. I don't know what media "anyone" follows. I don't know what organizations "anyone" belongs to. That's vital information, because getting free publicity in media that clients read, and speaking to organizations that prospects belong to, are among the most effective self-promotion strategies.

Use Varied Marketing Methods

Publicity and public speaking are just two of the dozens of no-cost techniques you can use to promote yourself.

Which of these strategies work for you will depend on whether you own your business, or work for one. In either case, there are many other moneymaking and moneysaving marketing options available to you as discussed in later chapters. But how you promote yourself is less important than that you promote yourself differently. You will never make a lasting impression if you use the same marketing methods as your competitors.

Low-Cost Ways to Promote Yourself

- Distribute evaluation forms that elicit referrals and testimonials.

- Network with "tipster" groups with members from different industries—or start one yourself.

- Create a newsletter for current, prospective, and ex-clients.

- Teach an adult education class.

- Develop an economical personal promotion kit, including a bio sheet, reprints of articles by and about you, testimonials, and lists of products, services, clients and references.

- Barter consultation time for personal photos, brochures, business cards, and other promotional services.

- Donate products or services to a community fundraising event.

- Communicate with prospects, clients and others via audiotaped or videotaped messages.

- "Work the crowd"—but not necessarily a booth—at a trade show.

- Offer and promote a "frequent buyers club."

- Distribute surveys and questionnaires among prospects.

- Conduct seminars for pros.

YOU ARE UNIQUE

We live in a day and age of great diversity and specialization in the workplace. The wonder is that so many people "market" themselves so similarly. Whatever their experience, specialized training, and daily responsibilities, they promote themselves the same way that everyone else does.

It's what others might call "Follow the Leader" marketing, but what I call "Follow the Follower" marketing. Its emphasis is on how most others, rather than just the leaders in the field, sell themselves.

There is no easier way to promote yourself than to play the "Same Game." Players don't try to blow their own horn in a unique way. They don't attempt to discover and describe their unique talents and abilities. They don't attempt to perceive the value in *being different*, nor try to promote their differences.

Same Game participants don't realize that self-promotion is important enough to be everybody's business. And how better to promote yourself than to share the things that are unique about you?

Sell Yourself First

Salespeople must sell themselves before they can sell their

products and services. Employees must promote themselves to supervisors if they expect to advance within the company. Entrepreneurs must market themselves before they can market their ideas to investors and, eventually, prospective clients. Executives must convince others of their leadership and management skills.

The fact is, *everyone* is different from everyone else. Yet very few attempt to demonstrate their differences. Few dare to be different in the manner in which they promote themselves.

> Anybody who is any good is different from anybody else.
> —Supreme Court Justice Felix Frankfurter

The Same Old "Stuff" Doesn't Work

If they promote themselves at all, so many professionals in so many industries use the same words to do so. They talk of themselves as "experienced" and "qualified" and "reliable." Chances are they use the same old methods to promote those words: résumés, cold calling, advertising, direct mail—and not much else.

How boring!

The good news is that players of the Same Game can harness all of their "follower" energy and rechannel it in a more useful direction. They can use it to discover their differences, create a truly unique "commercial," and develop unique ways to share it with those they believe should hear and understand it.

At first, this rechanneling doesn't come easily. We're not used to this idea of focusing on our differences. We may be more comfortable following the lead of others.

WHY BE DIFFERENT?

What, you ask, is wrong with your current strategy? Why *not* do as others do? Why *not* follow the lead of others when it comes to promoting ourselves? Surely, it's a lot easier to promote ourselves in the same way others in our field have promoted themselves. Why reinvent the self-marketing "wheel" when so many others before us have used the one already in place?

The problem with copying the marketing methods of others is that too many of those "others" want what we want.

A Crowded Marketplace

Rarely, if ever, is yours the only offer, proposal, recommendation, bid, application, plan, résumé, proposition, deal, or sales pitch. Too many others want to reach who you need to reach.

They target the same decision makers, and they use the same methods to get their attention. When you all use the same methods to reach the same people, no one can stand out as superior. And in a crowded marketplace, that's a recipe for failure.

The marketplace is cluttered with more than your competitors. Sometimes you have to meet and overcome unfavorable impressions of your profession, or deal with the baggage that competitors have left behind. Picture yourself as a sales trainer who is seeking a contract with a corporation that just fired another trainer because he failed to produce positive results. You would have to resell the company on the need and importance of training before attempting to sell the firm on yourself.

Can You Stand Out?

Another reason for you to promote yourself differently is the perception that many others do what you do.

At the very least, others have the same job title, have worked the same number of years, or are *perceived* to be as qualified. If these "others" haven't surfaced yet, they will. Competitors and challengers can come along at any time. Your client or customer can be approached by someone tomorrow, and you can be replaced next week.

Meeting *Their* Needs

Competitors want what you want, do what you do and try to reach the same target audience. How can you stand above the crowd? Your prospects, supervisors, and others are all tuned to the same radio station. Its call letters are WII-FM (What's in it for me?).

Oh, to be able to invest in that station! Its ratings must be extraordinary considering that all day, everyday, our clients, prospects and others we need to influence are listening.

It's your responsibility to create a personal commercial for their stations. There are many words you can choose for that commercial, but none packs as much punch as the word "only."

> Positioning is not what you do to a product. Positioning is what you do to the mind of the prospect.
> —Al Ries and Jack Trout,
> *Positioning: The Battle for Your Mind*

HARNESS THE POWER OF "ONLY"

"Only." What a word! It is the single word which can distinguish you from all the others who do what you do and want what you want. It puts you in a class by yourself, defining your "differentness" and signaling that you have what others lack.

Identify yourself as the only manufacturer with a public showroom, or the only financial

USP

In old sales and marketing training, you were generally told to develop your unique sales proposition, or USP. This is what makes you different and better for the customer. Newer work by Jack Trout and Al Ries has defined a broader concept.

POSITIONING

You want to position yourself in the minds of your prospects in a clear and distinct—different—way. This lets them know exactly how you can meet their needs better than others. It's a more complete way of focusing on your unique advantages.

officer with 20 years experience, or the firm's only bilingual attorney. When you set yourself apart, you prosper. Say that you are the *only* account executive in your area who has worked with "Fortune 500" companies, or the *only* scientist who has probed a rare tropical disease, or the *only* sales representative to lead the company six consecutive months. *That's* special.

If *only* I knew, in the early days of my business career, the power of the word "only!"

You, too, should find that power. Do what you must to develop your "onlyness." Create a list of what only you can do, and you will be able to do more than simply promote yourself. You will be able to appreciate yourself to a greater degree, and to overcome self-doubts more easily.

Don't Downgrade Yourself

Be advised that the same word that enables you to express your uniqueness can hinder you, as well. "Only" becomes a liability when you use it to mean "merely." "I'm only a government securities analyst," a woman told me following a workshop. "You can't expect *me* to market myself, can you?"

"Don't tell me you're 'only a securities analyst,'" I responded. "Begin the sentence by telling me you're 'the only securities analyst who _____.'"

Be Memorable

A communications specialist once told me that an individual typically remembers only one thing about another person several months after a chance meeting. That is the thing he or she will describe when recounting the meeting.

In other words, if I exchange business cards with a corporate executive at a networking session, the best I can count on is that he or she will remember one thing about me when recalling our meeting months later.

I want that one thing to be that I am "the *only* professional speaker in this area who gives motivational marketing programs that sell people on selling themselves differently." That, after all, is my commercial, my personal sales pitch that I want others to remember if they remember nothing else about me.

I was in Washington National Airport some time ago when I ran into a computer consultant whom I had met at a local networking function.

"You're the speaker, right?" she said. "The only one who talks about being different." She hadn't recalled the entire 25-word commercial I shared with her weeks before, but she did retain the key: my *only*. My mission had been accomplished.

You, too, should have a 25-word (or less) commercial that incorporates your "only." Sure, it's dandy if you have a four-color, 50-page, state-of-the-art marketing kit; a glossy, award-winning brochure, and a résumé that knocks their socks off. But, if and when someone is to remember you, or judge you, or tell someone else about you, it's that "only" commercial they will think of first.

SURVIVAL TACTICS

Restaurant Examples

Restaurants in this country have resorted to special events to differentiate themselves—and fill their tables. A Denver restaurant puts on dinners designed for cigar smokers, a Chicago establishment conducts olive oil tastings, a New Orleans eatery prepares special dinners for garlic lovers, and a smoke-free New York restaurant arranges special dinners (complete with smoked rabbit dumplings, duck ragout, and related items) to complement certain specialty beers.

Determine your "specialness," and you should be able to hold your own even against larger, more established competitors. For instance, the arrival of Domino's and Pizza Hut in Japan influenced some savvy local pizza outlets to develop and promote such unique varieties as apple or rice on pizza, German sausage and potato pizza with mayonnaise sauce, and shrimp in chili sauce on a sweetened pizza crust. They may not sound great to us, but they worked there.

Do those restaurants appeal to everybody? No. Are they unique? Yes.

> ### Answer This Question
>
> "Question No. 1 for the prospective business owner (should be): In 25 words or less, how is my concept (for a plumbing company or software house) notably different from that of others? If you can't succinctly explain how you're special to 'the man or woman on the street,' you're headed for trouble."
>
> —Tom Peters

"Unique Pancakes"

It was on a bicycle trip that I learned about the power of promoting your uniqueness.

In May of 1986 I set out with seven others to ride along the TransAmerica Bicycle Trail from Yorktown, Virginia, to Astoria, Oregon. I discovered that two central thoughts occupied my mind as I sat on a bike seat for ten hours a day, for 90 days, through ten states, over 4,500 miles: the condition of my rear end and the condition of my stomach.

The farther west we advanced, the more bikers we encountered and the more often the conversation centered on those two simple topics. It was especially important to me that I find the right food stops along the route. I ate at least eight times a day and still managed to lose 23 pounds during the trip.

Word-Of-Mouth Advertising Works

We were cycling through Kentucky when I first encountered an east-bound rider who recommended I visit "Paul and Paula's Pancake Palace" when I reached Western Kansas.

"When you get there, order the 'Biker's Biscuits' and the 'Pedaler's Pancakes,'" he said. "They're famous."

On four other occasions as we advanced through Illinois and Missouri I met bikers who suggested that I experience the biscuits and pancakes at "Paul and Paula's Pancake Palace." What was it about this place, I wondered, that it had cyclists buzzing a few states—and hundreds of miles—later?

The day finally arrived when I rode into that small western Kansas town and spotted the crowd of mostly bicyclists surrounding the cafe with the yellow sign on top that read: "Paul and Paula's Pancake Palace." The waiting line extended out the door and around the block.

Nearly an hour later, when I was finally seated, I had no doubt in my mind when the waitress asked for my order. "For weeks I've been hearing about your Pedaler's Pancakes and Biker's Biscuits," I said. "Better give me an order of each."

When the steaming plate arrived, it was with great anticipation that I dug into a pancake first, and then a biscuit. And it was with great disappointment that I realized that the pancakes tasted like, well, pancakes, and the biscuits had the flavor of biscuits I had tasted many times before.

I was miffed. I asked to meet the manager.

How Can Regular Pancakes Be Unique?

Minutes later, as I sat facing Paul across a cup of hot chocolate, I shared my curiosity. "I've heard so much about your Pedaler's Pancakes and Biker's Biscuits. Yet I found them to be pretty ordinary," I confessed. "How is it they're so famous and this place is so popular?"

"Some folks love 'em, some don't, but bikers come here by the hundreds every season," he said with a friendly smile. "That's because we're unique."

"Unique?"

"We're the only cafe that calls them 'Biker Biscuits' and 'Pedaler's Pancakes,'" he replied. "And we're the only cafe on the TransAm trail promoting itself as the only cafe that sells 'Biker Biscuits' and 'Pedaler's Pancakes.'"

"So?"

"It's a secret of success, friend. You can be successful, but you have to get ready first. And you can't get ready until you get different."

I pulled out of "Paul and Paula's Pancake Place" a few minutes later, doubting I would ever return but newly reminded of an important principal of self-promotion: Good things come to those who "get different."

More Uniqueness: Bed and Breakfasts

Various industries are daring to be different in their marketing in an effort to survive tough economic times. Proprietors of businesses from bed and breakfast inns to fishing tackle stores have tried anything and everything in recent years to stem an economic downturn.

There was an increase in the number of U.S. bed and breakfast establishments from 1,000 to 20,000 in the 10-year period ending in 1993, according to *The Wall Street Journal.* That, coupled with stiff competition from hard-pressed hotels and motels, has made for scarce profits in the B&B industry. To stay afloat, some proprietors began marketing features ranging from bathroom jacuzzis, to barnyard animals, to two-day courses on Chinese cooking.

"Nowadays, you have to do something different, something outrageous," said Barbara Notarius, a proprietor in Croton on Hudson, New York and the author of the book entitled *Open Your Own Bed and Breakfast.* "B&B owners have never had much marketing savvy, but now they realize they need to do something to stand out."

"Standing out" wasn't easy in her riverside community one hour outside of New York City. Local ordinances forbade her from posting a sign outside her house. To increase its exposure, Notarius hosted silent auctions and other community events, and converted her own room into a $250 per night honeymoon suite.

"We got ourselves written up in a publication called 'The Best Places to Kiss in New York,' and the room was booked every weekend," she said.

Other B&B's promoted sports club privileges, bus tour packages, and more to compete with hotels and motels that slashed rates and offered complimentary breakfasts, concierge service, express check-in, no-smoking rooms, personal computers and day care.

Fishing for Differences

The fishing tackle industry also encountered hard times in the early 1990s, thanks in large part to the aggressive expansion into the marketplace of such discounters as Wal-Mart, Kmart, and sports superstores. That, plus the 11 percent decline in the number of people fishing in the three-year period ending in 1993, forced many independent retailers to close their doors.

But others "dared to be different" to stay in business. They offered new and different services and products that the all-purpose discounters didn't. For the Salmon Stop in Waukegan, Illinois, "different" meant promoting a community program to get children "hooked on fishing, not on drugs," and supplying fishing gear for a local family fishing event that drew dozens of new customers into the shop.

For Quaker Lane Bait & Tackle Ltd. in North Kingstown, Rhode Island, "different" in the early 1990s meant adding a service to repair trolling motors, rods, and reels. By 1993, the company earned profit margins of more than 100 percent on its repair work, and total sales exceeded $1 million.

Other retailers marketed seminars on topics like basic fishing for children and how to hook a big fish.

"The independents that were left after the Wal-Marts moved into the business had to fight back," recalled Bob Vickers, editor of the *The Fishing Tackle Trade News.* "They had to push their knowledge—of where to fish locally, and what lures to use. And they had to make themselves different from the big guys by selling things like soft goods."

Vickers said marketwise, tackle shops lured customers with special discounts on tackle, and then sold them other items such as tee shirts and caps at a considerable mark up.

It Pays to Be Different

Other service providers have used innovative marketing in recent years to overcome stiff competition. Carwashes have promoted such on-site entertainment as rabbit petting zoos, aquariums, sun decks, cable TV and video games. Laundromats have offered inside restaurants, tanning salons, exercise rooms and playgrounds.

Owners of bed and breakfast establishments, fishing tackle shops, carwashes and laundramats may not have much else in common, but in challenging economic times they must embark on a similar mission. They must define what *only* they can do, and what they alone can offer that competitors can't or don't.

Deliver your "only" message in person or in print. Your "only" belongs on your letterhead, bio sheet, business cards, and brochures, with your secretary and on your voice mail.

Getting Your Price

The importance of your "only" transcends a verbal commercial, a voicemail message or a tagline on stationery. How you communicate your "only" can determine the fees you charge and the amount of money you earn.

You can maintain your price if you can distinguish yourself from others who charge less. You can distinguish your company by your "only" statement. Are you the only firm that guarantees its work? The only one offering free delivery, or free replacement parts or "frequent buyer" privileges? The only one that has been in business for 15 years, or has been honored for its service?

Decide what sets you apart, and you shouldn't have to play with your prices. You should be able to steer clear of the no-price-is-too-low reputation that organizations get when they constantly slash their fees. You should be able to rise above the undercutting game that so many play, and no one wins.

By being unique, you can maintain fee integrity even in the toughest of times. But you need to communicate that you are different from all of the others, and that you offer benefits that others can't.

Interior Designers Fight Price Wars

Interior designers in Omaha have confronted severe price competition for years. They are quick to blame the Nebraska Furniture Mart. The Mart  has showroom space exceeding that of several football fields. It is the largest privately-owned facility of its kind in the United States. It sells everything from futons to fabrics at prices well below those that local designers would charge if they bought the items wholesale and sold them to customers.

Some prospects even seek advice from local designers, only to purchase the items on their own from the Mart and save on the designers' commissions. Similarly, some consumers have taken the free advice and ordered the products through a discount catalog.

They Can't Win on Price

Local designers have complained about the difficulty of getting a fair price for their services and about the pressure to cut their fees to hang on to customers. The designers spent considerable time and energy grousing about—but participating in—a price war. Fee cutting became, for many, the rule rather than the exception.

When I began working with Nebraska designers, I discovered that they were experts on the local price wars. They knew more about price undercutting than about self-promotion. Few could explain what made them different. Few could list services or benefits that they alone could offer. Few could explain why prospects should work with them rather than shopping through the Mart or discount catalogues.

I devoted an entire workshop to persuading those designers to rechannel their "seige mentality" and price war energy into self-promotion. I urged them to write marketing messages defining their differences, and spelling out benefits that they offered exclusively. I recommended that they promote the value of their expertise.

"You may get lower prices elsewhere, but you won't get me" was the approach I recommended they use with their prospects. Substantiate that claim, I told them, and you will be able to maintain the integrity of your fees.

Marketing Unique Baseball

Skilled self-promoters understand the value of promoting their unique message *uniquely*.

Take the case of Lindsey Nelson, the radio announcer for the New York Mets in 1962, their first and worst season. The team was to lose a total of 120 games that year, prompting manager Casey Stengel at one point to inquire: "Can't anybody here play this game?"

Nelson sought a way to attract attention to the pathetic team—and network attention to himself. He began to show up at games in psychedelic sports coats, hardly standard wearing apparel for broadcasters of the day. The gawdy jackets—of which Nelson eventually owned 700—became legendary, and so did Lindsey Nelson, even though he was the voice of one of baseball's worst teams in history.

More recently, professional baseball has witnessed another example of unique marketing.

Hoping to boost attendance and merchandise sales, minor league baseball teams in recent years have adopted a new approach to promotion and marketing. Several teams decided to drop the names of their parent clubs and adopt unusual substitutes.

"I don't care what you do," campaign strategist James Carville once advised presidential candidate Bill Clinton. "But just make damn sure it's big and different."

"Teams with the same name as their parent clubs have nothing to sell," Al Mangum, the general manager of the Durham, N.C. Bulls, explained. "All they have is a duplicate of their logo."

Prior to the 1993 season, the minor league team in Cedar Rapids, Iowa changed its name from "Reds" to "Kernels." Accompanying the change: a stylish new logo of a baseball sprouting from a corn husk. Within three months, the team sold more than $20,000 in souvenirs, about half the total of the entire previous year.

As soon as the Carolina Mudcats moved from Columbus, Georgia and changed their name from the Astros, their cap and other merchandise sales soared. The team, now based in Zebulon, N.C., adopted a logo featuring a whiskered catfish poking its head through the letter "C". The result: 1992 souvenir sales of nearly $500,000, more than double the 1989 total. That, despite the team's dismal 1992 record of 52–92.

Clearly, the teams discovered the wisdom of thinking big—and differently.

Uniqueness in Love

In 1954, Robert Brachman, a 30-year-old sales representative in Milwaukee, knew he had to do something different if he was to win back his 24-year-old former girlfriend.

"We had a disagreement, and she told me I was an immature, spendthrift playboy," Brachman recalls. "She told me never to call her again. I was heartsick."

Robert had done some creative wooing. He had shown up at her doorstep with a used car he bought for her, only to be told that her father wouldn't allow her to accept it. He hid a pecan pie—her favorite—in a downtown locker and mailed her the key, along with a variety of scavenger hunt clues to help her find it. She told him his crazy "frivolous antics" were wasting his time—and hers.

"When she refused to talk to me any more, I knew I had to get her attention," Brachman says. "So I kept thinking of even more imaginative things that would make her think of me as more interesting than others."

The most imaginative of his efforts involved renting space for $20 per week on the billboard near the downtown department store where she worked as a sportswear buyer. For seven weeks, until he ran out of money, Brachman ran poetic billboard appeals to his lost Arlene. One, incorporating expressions that she once used, read:

> "Swellsy, Dandy, Peachy Keen
> Why, Oh Why, Are You So Mean?"

Uniqueness Attracts Publicity

The billboard courtship immediately caught the interest of *The Milwaukee Journal*, which carried a front page story on it. The nation's wire services quickly caught on, and hundreds of newspapers worldwide ran stories with headlines like: "She Wouldn't Listen: He Rents Billboard;" "Jilted, He Woos Arlene by Billboard;" and "Mean Arlene Lets Swain Foot Bills."

Letters poured in from across the country. The billboard company, initially skeptical of the legality of his plan, called to encourage him to rent more space and post more messages. A national bus company offered to transport the couple anywhere in the United States, if Arlene agreed to marry him. A Canadian railroad offered a honeymoon trip.

The unique courtship which captured the nation's attention finally caught Arlene's too. After turning down 12 proposals, she finally agreed to marry him. They have been happily married and living in the Milwaukee area ever since, glad to this day that he persisted and "dared to be different" in his pursuit.

BE FLEXIBLE

Thinking differently requires something of a "midcourse correction." Chances are you didn't learn in childhood to concentrate on your "differentness." You didn't take courses on being different, and may have learned instead to conform to be accepted by others.

Try to recall an instance when, as a youngster, you sought a special privilege. Perhaps it was an extra helping of milk and cookies, or permission to be first in line or the opportunity to stay out longer during recess. How often would the teacher respond by saying: "Just who do you think you are? What makes *you* so special?"

The better you become at defining and refining your answers to those questions, the more focused you will become. That focus will increase your chances of fulfilling your goals and reaching the level of success that you envision.

That midcourse correction in your thinking will send you on your way to the top. Be wary of others, however, who may try to block your progress en route.

Risk Leads to Rewards

By taking the risk of promoting yourself uniquely, you will win the greatest rewards. That's because you'll "win" even if you fail to accomplish your immediate goal. Sell yourself differently from others and you may at least impress someone in a way that will help you to "connect" the next time an opportunity arises.

Fail to differentiate yourself, and you make no impression. *That* could be the biggest risk of all.

IT'S SAFER TO BE DIFFERENT

Strive to promote yourself differently, and you will improve your chances for a safe and secure future. Strive, instead, for "safety," and financial security may elude you.

You may think that you're playing it safe by choosing not to promote yourself, or by playing the "Same Game" of self-promotion. In fact, by doing so you lose your sense of purpose. Reliquish control of your career to fate, and your future will be determined by chance, not choice.

Self-promotion is an exercise in self-growth. It requires you to identify your positives, differentiate yourself from others, and package yourself accordingly. Practice pays off. The more experience you get in pinpointing your special abilities, the

How Earl Nightingale Became One of the Most Successful Radio Commentators in History

 Shortly after getting his first announcing job at KTAR Radio in Phoenix, Earl Nightingale tried to elevate himself to bigger and better things. His fellow broadcasters teased him about his attempts to promote himself to the network level.

Nightingale later recalled how he gave "so much pizzazz to the local commercials—whether for the local mortuary or sporting goods store—that my announcer friends soon dubbed me 'network' and kidded me and found my efforts ludicrous." When Nightingale announced his plans in 1949 to buy a one-way ticket to Chicago to seek employment with network radio, the other announcers responded with "unbelieving stares and vociferous arguments" why his efforts would fail.

But his self-promotion efforts paid off. In Chicago, CBS-affiliate WBBM offered him a network contract that, he said, gave him "more money that I had dreamed of earning."

Nightingale took what others considered a risk by moving to Chicago and promoting himself as a network-caliber announcer. By daring to be different, he pursued what turned out to be a much more secure career course than if he had stayed in Phoenix. He became one of the most successful announcers and commentators in network radio history.

more adept you will become at demonstrating how and why you stand out.

There is a far more substantial risk in *not* marketing yourself. In the words of hockey star Wayne Gretzky: "You miss 100 percent of the shots you never take."

Those who attempt to promote themselves differently take responsibility for their lives. Those who don't, shirk that responsibility.

THE "YOU" THAT YOU'RE SELLING

Who *are* you, anyway, and why should others care? What makes *you* so special?

Appreciate Yourself

Knowing you're special isn't enough. You have to give yourself credit for it, as well.

It is so easy to take ourselves for granted, and fail to give credit where credit is due. You may know people who can drone on for hours about their shortcomings, faults and failures. It's as if they have become experts on the topic of their inadequacies. Funny how those same "experts" can contribute so little information about their attributes and personal successes. Perhaps they don't have time to ponder the subject, preoccupied as they are with negative thoughts about themselves.

> The best things in life are yours if you can appreciate yourself. That's the way to stop worrying and start living.
>
> —Dale Carnegie

There is special joy in savoring the flavor of your daily accomplishments. Only by learning to experience that joy can you graduate from the ranks of the "striver" to become an "arriver." You can't excel at self-promotion until you make that transformation.

Project Your "Specialness"

Arrivers give the impression that they *already* have won. Their attitudes, mannerisms, and words communicate that they have reached the top of their professions. They exude confidence and serenity. Arrivers are leaders who look, act, and talk the part of those who are successful, and are proud of it.

Play the part of the arriver, and you will stand out from the multitudes. You will establish yourself as someone who is different and special.

Self-appreciation is the foundation of self-promotion. Not until you fully understand your unique qualities and special talents are you ready to dare to be different in the way you promote yourself.

VISIBILITY AND CREDIBILITY

Setting yourself apart from your competitors will increase your visibility and credibility. It will give you a competitive edge. It will bolster your self-confidence, and help you understand and appreciate your uniqueness. It will get you the recognition and rewards that you deserve.

Whoever you are, whatever you do, you're too good to be your own best secret. You have worked too hard for too long to go unrecognized.

Not only do you have so much to gain by promoting your uniqueness, but you have virtually nothing to lose.

Take Inventory

Sit down in a quiet place some day soon, and compile a list of your:

- attributes
- capabilities
- most admired traits
- skills
- qualifications
- areas of expertise
- most recent personal and professional accomplishments
- greatest personal and professional accomplishments
- awards and honors
- success stories
- record of overcoming obstacles
- record of mastering challenges
- contributions to your organization and profession
- career milestones

Review your list carefully, and periodically add to it. Where appropriate, insert superlatives that indicate how you stand out. Indicate, for example, if you are the *most* experienced, or the *highest* ranking, or the recipient of the *most* honors. Your list should convince you, if you are not convinced already, that you really *are* special.

- You won't lose money, since some of the most effective self-promotion strategies—like free publicity—cost the least.
- You won't lose time, because a period spent differentiating and distinguishing yourself is time well spent.

Perhaps all you *will* lose is your anonymity. That loss can only result in an understanding and respect from others for who you are and what you do.

The Dare-to-Be-Different Challenge

Accepting the challenge to promote yourself in a unique way assures that you will take responsibility and control over your career. It frees you from the "follow the follower" restraints of the "Same Game." It also prevents you from blaming your shortcomings on the economy, clients, competitors, age, or just plain bad luck.

Accepting the challenge to be different enables you to look into the mirror each day and *believe* yourself when you say: "What is to be is up to me." Accepting the challenge means that you dare to share your differentness.

Consider yourself challenged.

- **I dare you** to be different in the words you choose to use about yourself and your company or organization.
- **I dare you** to be different in selecting your target audience, and deciding who it is that you need to influence.
- **I dare you** to be different in the methods you use to communicate your message.

It Works

Accept these dares, and you will discover the most important secret of self-promotion: your differences are your diamonds. Believe in that

> Daring ideas are like chessmen. Moved forward, they may be beaten, but they may start a winning game.
>
> —Goethe

secret, and you will discover the magic of reaching a higher level of personal achievement, income and success than you ever thought possible.

BURST INTO ACTION

Start by doing what's necessary; then do what's possible; and suddenly you are doing the impossible.

—St. Francis of Assisi

The Dare-To-Be-Different Checklist

Work toward promoting yourself differently, and you will discover new and different rewards. Begin by following these guidelines:

1 SAY DIFFERENT THINGS ABOUT YOURSELF. Emphasize your "onlys."

2 THINK DIFFERENTLY. Focus on today, rather than yesterday or tomorrow.

3 ACT DIFFERENTLY. Give the impression that you already are successful.

4 SOUND DIFFERENTLY. Talk the talk of an "arriver," rather than a "striver."

5 LOOK DIFFERENT. Take on an appearance that distinguishes you from others.

6 SELL YOUR SERVICES DIFFERENTLY. Spell out their unique benefits.

7 OFFER SOMETHING DIFFERENT. Make available options that others don't.

8 GUARANTEE SOMETHING DIFFERENTLY. Back up your services in a way that others don't.

9 TARGET DIFFERENTLY. Pursue a different niche in the market.

10 COMMUNICATE DIFFERENTLY. Get your message across in a unique way.

11 FOLLOW UP DIFFERENTLY. Stay in touch in ways in which clients are unaccustomed.

Do all that, and you will discover how being different makes a difference.

WHAT IS YOUR CUSTOMER
Really BUYING?

Noulan W. Bowker

Noulan W. Bowker, Certified Management Consultant, has been providing marketing, consulting, market research, and training services as an independent contractor since 1990. His clients are mainly companies who sell advanced technology products for industrial, commercial, or government customers in global markets.

Mr. Bowker has a 30-year track record of practical experience in industrial marketing, international sales, channel development, management, engineering, consulting, and training. Over his career, he has worked for over 45 organizations, as either an employee or a consultant. His business experience spans 23 countries in North America, Europe, and Asia.

Graduating as an electronics engineer in 1971, Mr. Bowker taught engineering in Thailand for two years. From that time onward, his employers and consulting clients have been rapidly growing, leading-edge advanced technology companies with global markets. They include Digital Equipment Corporation with computers; MacDonald Dettwiler, with satellite remote sensing; Statpower Technologies with power inverters; ACL Software with software for auditors; and Brooks Automation, with equipment and software for making semiconductors.

Noulan W. Bowker, N. Bowker Inc., 2625 Mahon Avenue, North Vancouver, BC V7N 3S7, Canada; phone (604) 980-4494; fax: (604) 980-4461; e-mail noulan@nbowker.com; Internet www.nbowker.com.

WHAT IS YOUR CUSTOMER *Really* BUYING?

Noulan W. Bowker

A purchase decision is not a decision to buy an item
. . . but a decision to enter a bonded relationship . . . .
This requires of the would-be seller a new orientation
and a new strategy.

—Tom Peters

I n the mid-1980s I bought a sailing school and
yacht charter business on the West Coast.

As serious sailors, my partners and I were
initially attracted to this business by the technical
excellence of the sailing courses and the number
and quality of boats offered for charter. Prior to the
purchase, I interviewed a number of the company's
recent customers to find out what was important
to them about sailing and how the company
might improve its sailing courses and charter
operations.

THE ROMANCE OF SAILING

To my surprise, the vast majority of customers told me that the most important thing for them was the opportunity to socialize. It became obvious that the real reason they ventured into sailing was to meet new people and develop friendships, particularly of the romantic variety. Taking the sailing courses would lead not only to obtaining a skipper's certificate, but also hopefully to the possibility of finding the perfect "first mate."

The business had not previously catered to this need, even though it had a large and attractive facility in a popular area of the waterfront. Upon taking over the business in the fall, we started a sailing club and held parties every couple of weeks throughout the winter. Starting early in the spring, we organized weekend flotilla cruises, assigning four to six participants per boat so they could meet new people while sharing the charter costs. For the first time in the company's history, cash flow was positive throughout the winter, and spring charters increased substantially.

We quickly learned that the key to success with sailing lessons and yacht charters was realizing that we were actually in the romantic matchmaking business. Even though what we did and talked about was sailing, we were actually just setting the scene for the truly important stuff that was happening on our boats and in the clubhouse.

What do your customers value the most in your offerings? Those are the elements that should define your business.

AN EXPANDED CONCEPT OF "THE PRODUCT"

Inventing the Whole Product for Customers

In reinventing our sailing business to provide what most of our customers really wanted to buy, we had to provide a variety of extra support services. By adding social activities to the product concept, we were able to expand beyond our limited market of hard-core sailors to embrace many more people who would enjoy sailing.

> Quality in a service or product is not what you put into it. It is what the client or customer gets out of it.
>
> —Peter F. Drucker

Similarly, as a marketing and salesperson for technical products, I found that most of my customers could seldom use the product in the form initially conceived by the engineers. To make the first sales, I had to find a few adventurous customers and help them develop the technical and organizational processes to make practical use of the product.

We usually had to add a number of features to the basic design and provide additional services. Also, we had to specify additional equipment and services to either be supplied by the customer or be purchased from other suppliers. Only after we had solved all of these problems would the majority of the market be willing to buy our product. Customers like to buy solutions, not problems.

In other words, we had to invent the application *and* the collection of additional goods and services needed to implement it—we had to create the "Whole Product."

CUSTOMERS AND TARGET MARKETS

Prior to looking at more complex examples, let us clarify what we mean by the term "customer" and "market." In this chapter, what I really mean by "the customer" is a person or organization that is representative of all the customers and prospects in your target market. A market is a group of customers who reference each other when buying. This definition appeals to me because it is framed from customers' perceptions of the product and the markets they are in.

Typhoon Tracking in Asia

I was fortunate, early in my career, to be challenged with marketing and selling MDA's very complex satellite ground stations to the governments of developing countries. One of these products was a new generation of stations for receiving pictures from weather satellites.

Selling this device to developing countries involved a steep learning curve for MDA because it had previously sold only to the Canadian government—a very knowledgeable customer with considerable internal technical resources. Fortunately, from having worked in Thailand for the two years following my graduation in engineering, I had some understanding of the levels of technical expertise and infrastructure we might expect with customers from developing nations.

Because these new customers needed a lot of help to acquire, install, and use this equipment, we had to provide extra equipment and services for them to be able to use our product.

The company originally sent out promotional literature on the equipment in response to interest expressed by the meteorological departments of a number of countries, many of which were in Asia. This literature mainly provided detailed descriptions of the electronic equipment and software features and specifications. When I started visiting my prospective customers, I quickly realized that they did not understand the literature describing our technical wizardry. Even more important, they didn't care to!

Hope: The Hidden Component in Every Product

When you read a catalog, you find descriptions of what each product is made of. It's 100% cotton, or it's solid steel, or it's extruded plastic.

In order to sell the items, however, you must include a big dash of hope. You can't touch hope or see it, but it has to be there because that's what customers buy.

People buy an appliance because hope tells them it will save them some time. They buy a service because it gives them the hope that it will improve a situation.

If the built-in hope satisfies the buyer's image of what a product should do, something else develops: faith. That's even better. It means a customer is likely to buy anything with that company's name on it.

—Theodore Levitt,
The Marketing Imagination

These customers were meteorologists who were interested in the product only because it would allow them to analyze and predict the movement of typhoons more reliably. For them, the product was a typhoon tracker. Once we realized that we were really in the typhoon tracking business, we adjusted our product concept and were able to capture almost all of these opportunities.

THE WHOLE PRODUCT MODEL

In an effort to organize my thinking, I developed the Whole Product Model. I have found it to be useful for teaching management classes and in helping my clients develop practical product and marketing strategies.

Only in dealing with Whole Products for your customers can you sell what your customers want to buy. The nine-component Whole Product model, illustrated in Figure 1 on the next page, serves as a checklist for all of the elements that must be supplied by you, your partners, and the customer to complete the Whole Product.

Note that the components are grouped according to their primary sources.

- **Internally sourced elements.** The Core Product, the Support Services, and the Product Road Map components are provided exclusively by your company and are under your complete control.

- **Jointly sourced elements**. Trust is the most important aspect of your rela-

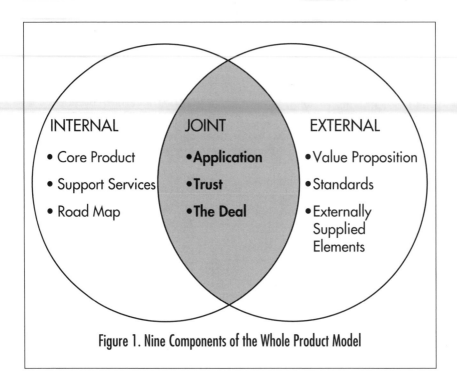

Figure 1. Nine Components of the Whole Product Model

tionship. The Application is developed and supplied jointly with your customer. The Deal is a joint understanding and document.

- **Externally sourced elements**. The Value Proposition, comprising the customer's values and evidence criteria, originates with the customer. Standards come from outside your company and you must respond to them. Externally Supplied items are goods and services that are necessary for the application, but will be provided by the customer or other suppliers.

In the sailing school example, our Core Product was a set of services comprising sailing lessons and boat charters. The Application component was the sailing club and the flotilla cruise program, a synthesis of our sailing services and the social lives of our customers.

In the weather satellite station example, our Core Product was a system comprising several boxes filled with state-of-the-art electronics and software. The Application was typhoon tracking. In order for the customer to get this capability with our equipment, we had to supply a number of additional goods and services to provide the necessary Whole Product.

For example, although the customers were meteorologists, they needed to learn how to use the new digital enhancement capabilities that made our product such a powerful tool for analyzing and predicting the behavior of typhoons. As part of the project, we had to arrange several months of on-the-job training for them in North America at a government weather satellite station that used our equipment.

---

3 Keys to Using the Whole Product Model Approach

The three keys to using the Whole Product Model approach are:

1 Look at the product from the customer's point of view.

2 Understand the Application (what the customer is *really* buying).

3 To ensure the customer gets everything needed, use all nine components of the model as a checklist.

THE 9 COMPONENTS OF THE WHOLE PRODUCT MODEL

1 **THE CORE PRODUCT.** The Core Product is what we normally think of as being The Product or The Service. In the case of a manufactured product, it is what your factory makes and ships out to the customer. In our sailing business, the Core Product was the service of providing sailing lessons and boat charters. The core competency, proprietary technology, and key competitive advantages of the product generally reside in the Core Product component.

Product Identity

Even though we know that the Application is really what the customer is buying, customers typically perceive the Core Product to be the product. Also, companies normally identify themselves as suppliers of the Core Product. In the satellite station example, even though the meteorologists were really buying typhoon tracking, they would identify the product as a satellite receiving station.

Standardization and Customization

Customers like to feel that your product or service is "for them." The challenge is to design it to meet the unique requirements of each customer, while minimizing costs through as much standardization as possible.

I was lucky to start my marketing career at Digital Equipment Corporation in a business group that developed a clever way to meet this goal. It offered a modular approach. By being able to easily assemble highly customized systems from standard modules, we could sell at a very competitive price. This is a general approach that I have found to be very successful in many businesses.

Often the desired customization can be most easily and economically provided through the other eight product components.

Customization Sells

Every customer wants something "just for them." Look for customer services and products to offer existing buyers. Develop customization by:

1. Making customers your design partners.

2. Standardizing the parts that go into each service or product.

3. Looking for smaller markets, not bigger ones.

For instance, if you give seminars, have modules that cover various topics that you can mix in different ways for each market.

—*Executive Edge* newsletter

---

2 **THE APPLICATION.** The Application is a synthesis of your technology and your customer's technology as illustrated in Figure 2. It is the essence of the product from your customer's point of view.

Understanding your customer's Application and ensuring that it is successfully implemented are perhaps the most important aspects of your product strategy.

Distributors as Customers

If you are selling products through external distribution, it is important to realize that the distributor is also a customer whose application is simply the business proposition of buying and reselling your product.

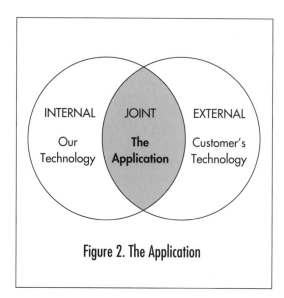

Figure 2. The Application

Organizations as Customers

With an organizational customer, each department or person can view the product differently because they want different benefits. A quality control manager would see new factory equipment as a quality application whereas a vice president of marketing might see it as a means of producing a more competitive product.

3 **VALUE PROPOSITION.** The Value Proposition is how your customers value your product on their terms. They may value it in dollars or according to less tangible criteria, ranging from private personal values to published corporate values. Decisions to select and keep you as a supplier are based on how well you measure up to their values compared to the competition. There are two parts to the Value Proposition:

1. The Values (your customer's values and their order of priority)

2. The Evidence Criteria (how customers measure your product against their values)

In the case of selling weather satellite stations in Asia, almost any improvement in the early warning of typhoons would help reduce the great loss of life and property. In addition, this application had good propaganda value for the politicians. People seeing the weather satellite pictures on TV weather reports would be regularly reminded how well their government was serving them. The Value Proposition of this product allowed the governments in the region to readily justify the large purchase budgets required.

> ### Values of Organizations
>
> When your customer is an organization, there are three types of values and evidence criteria that you will encounter:
> 1. Objective Values
> 2. Professional Values
> 3. Personal Values

Objective Values. Values and the Evidence Criteria are often partly expressed in financial terms. For example, with capital equipment purchases, calculations such as return on investment, months for payback, or savings in operating costs may be considered.

Professional Values. The values and evidence criteria of individuals that relate to their job functions or professions are somewhat predictable in analyzing the characteristics of a market. For example, one can predict that a controller will value cost reduction and a personnel manager will value improved working conditions.

Personal Values. Much has been done recently to profile the personal value systems of consumers based on socioeconomic and geographic classifications. Things get complicated when people in your customer's organization make decisions about your company or product based on personal values.

This is probably more the rule than the exception. The best way to handle this from a strategic point of view is to make sure that delivery of the Trust component of the Whole Product includes sufficient personal contact with customers.

Cultural Values. Values can vary significantly by organization and geography.

The culture of an organization may affect its buying decisions. In Europe, and especially in Asia, I have found that more value is placed on the continuity of personal relationships in business than in North America. I have had many offshore customers and distributors complain to me that they have a limited trust in North American companies because they frequently must adjust to dealing with new people.

Evidence Criteria. It is important to understand your customers' Evidence Criteria. For example, in the weather satellite station example, the customer's personnel greatly valued the opportunity to travel to North America, for both personal and professional reasons. Overseas travel was typically beyond their personal means and it greatly enhanced their status. To meet their Evidence Criteria, the contract had to specify clearly and in detail exactly who would be trained, where, for how long, and what expenses were to be paid.

> ## Two Key Questions for Determining the Value Proposition
>
> **1** What is important to you about...? (to elicit values)
>
> **2** How will you know when you have it? (to elicit evidence criteria)

4 **SUPPORT SERVICES.** Often, your Support Services are more important to satisfying the customer's needs than your basic Product.

Customers often expect Support Services, either because they are listed in the contract or because they are provided as common practice to your market. Examples of such services are installation, warranty, training, and telephone support. You may supply these directly or through partners such as distributors.

5 **STANDARDS.** The number of standards and their importance for suppliers has increased greatly over the last few years.

It is important to identify the standards that might apply to your product in all its potential markets early in the design stage. Often it can be expensive or impossible to modify a product to comply with new standards after it is in production.

Technical and industry standards often work in your favor because they reduce costs of compatibility with other products and enhance marketability. For example, compliance with the ISO-9001 quality assurance standard is important for credibility in certain markets.

What Is ISO Certification?

ISO-9000, 14000, etc. is a system of standards developed by the International Organization for Standardization (ISO).

Many manufacturing executives say ISO certification gives them a competitive advantage in doing business, especially in the European community.

—American Society for Quality Control

Some regulatory standards pose problems for suppliers. They tend to vary wildly among political jurisdictions, even within North America, and obtaining compliance certification can be lengthy and costly.

6 EXTERNALLY SUPPLIED ITEMS. You will be relying on your customer to supply at least some facilities, equipment, consumables, services, or expertise in order for your application to function. Customer-supplied elements can range from a simple power outlet to a complex industrial process to be implemented on your equipment

Local distributors may provide important goods or services for the application, such as local installation, training, or warranty service. A critical contribution required of the customer for most applications is personnel who are skilled and knowledgeable enough to be able to operate and maintain the product.

Why should you be concerned about elements that are the responsibility of the customer or others to supply? Failure of the customer or a partner to provide adequate facilities, people, or ser-

Take Charge

Assume accountability for the customer getting all externally supplied items, even though you are not required to do so. Planning ahead will not only minimize the associated costs, but will also allow you to account for them in your risk analysis, product costing, and pricing.

vices has been a major source of frustration and lost profitability for manufacturers. When the product "doesn't work," the manufacturer is often blamed, even when the source of the problem is the customer or local partner.

You can start to protect yourself by ensuring that the contracts with your customer and partners include comprehensive lists of exactly what each party must provide and when. Then, follow up to confirm that their contributions are being completed on schedule. Think of this process as a project that you must manage.

7 **THE DEAL.** The Deal includes the price and all the commercial terms and conditions of the sale, such as the payment schedule, delivery time, the warranty period, and a complete list of what both the supplier and the customer will provide and do. It is prudent to be very cautious about any verbal commitments from organizational customers. Record both their verbal commitments and yours, and then provide them with a copy. The person you dealt with may change jobs and, without this documentation, his replacement may not honor the arrangement.

Although the price is important, sometimes other factors, such as delivery time or payment terms, can be just as important financially to you or your customer.

An important lesson I have learned is that different people can have quite different ideas about exactly what a particular deal is, especially when you are selling to people from different cultures. The value in having a written contract is to ensure clarity of the understanding, not to have a document to litigate over if something goes wrong. Consider it to be a partnership agreement.

Unlike North Americans, some cultures (in Asia, for example) do not place a high value on written contracts. Instead, their intention may be to rely on renegotiating the deal if circumstances should change to their disadvantage. The way to deal with this possibility is to budget for travel and time to maintain close relationships with such customers, so that any difficulties can be detected early and can be resolved in a win-win manner.

8 TRUST. As the supplier, you are responsible for building and maintaining a relationship of mutual trust with your customers. Many products now are so complex that we must rely on the continued support of the manufacturer for the life of the product. I remember successfully maintaining and tuning up my 1961 Volvo when I was a student. However, I would never attempt to fix anything under the hood of my new Explorer. I must trust the people at my local Ford dealership for service.

Corporations increasingly rely on suppliers to provide higher levels of support for most types of products. Companies are moving to closer and longer lasting supplier relationships because the costs of evaluating and adjusting to new products are so high. Customers need to have a high level of trust with their suppliers before they will relinquish direct control over important operational functions of their businesses.

Rapport Builds Trust. Real trust ultimately comes from developing rapport with individuals— a feeling of familiarity and predictability. People do not really trust organizations—they trust individuals. Rapport comes from direct contact—the closer and more frequent, the better.

Rapport comes largely from a person's feeling that the other person is like them. This is another critical reason for investigating your customer's application and business in detail, learning its jargon and how people in that industry think.

> There's a world of choice out there. People are looking for products they can trust, not just ones that meet their needs.
>
> —Lou Pritchett,
> *Stop Paddling and Start Rocking the Boat*

With the high personnel turnover in North American businesses, it pays to have a procedure in place to ensure that regular contact is maintained with the key people in customer organizations and rapport is re-established with any replacements. For instance, all major accounts can have a top executive and a service rep assigned. Turnover in service reps can be bridged by the top exec.

Rapport Across Cultures. People in many cultures outside of North America find it difficult to approach or accept someone without an introduction from a mutual acquaintance. An introduction is simply a transfer of rapport. (Also see Chapter 8 on referrals.) Developing good rapport with people from different cultures is more difficult because the "sameness" factor is less. One of the most important jobs of local distributors or representatives is to help you deliver the trust component of the product, by obtaining and maintaining rapport with your customers, and transferring it to your people when required.

A Customer-Oriented Culture. At Digital Equipment, one very effective way we developed the trust with our prospects and customers was by inviting them to visit the factory floor and talk to anyone. This unrestricted access was considered to be too risky elsewhere in the computer industry. It worked at Digital because all employees felt individually responsible for doing the best possible job for their customers. Another very effective relationship and trust builder at Digital was its user group, whose members were all end users. Customers liked to participate because they obtained valuable informa-

---

All of Us Can Sell Better Than One of Us

Invite your prospects to visit your company. You should be able to establish more credibility in that one visit than a salesperson could in dozens of calls.

You may even take it one step further. If you know your competitor's plant would not impress your prospects, suggest they visit it. It's important for them to be able to make their own comparisons.

—Clifton J. Reichard, director of business development, Ball Corp.

tion from each other for implementing their applications. Digital's customer-oriented culture was great for building relationships and trust.

9 THE ROAD MAP. The Product Road Map is your plan for developing new or improved products. In the other eight components, the model describes the whole product at any instant of time. The Road Map describes how it changes over time. These days, many businesses must change their product lines almost continuously to meet evolving customer needs, to remain competitive, to reduce costs, to accommodate new customers, or to provide additional applications to current customers.

Your Product Road Map is often a very important component of the product for your customers. They have invested a great deal to evaluate your product and your company. They want assurance that they will be able to take advantage of technological improvements and add additional capabilities in the future without having to switch suppliers.

Even if your core product remains the same, other components of the whole product will normally evolve over the product life cycle. As Geoffrey Moore described in his book *Crossing the Chasm,* "Innovator" and some "Early Adopter" customers will be willing to buy the Core Product and do all or most of the application development themselves. The bulk of the market, however, starting with the "Early Majority," will expect and need all of the components of the Whole Product. Referencing the model, we can see that failure of a company to "cross the chasm" is often due to insufficient development of the application and failure to provide all of the nine product components that are needed to satisfy the Value Proposition of its Early Majority market.

Process beats substance . . . The rhythm of the unfolding relationship, the way you are handled (informed, misinformed, belatedly informed, not informed) explains more about how you react to a product or service than the so-called result itself.
—Tom Peters

USING THE 9 COMPONENTS AS A CHECKLIST

The following story illustrates the value of using the nine whole-product components as a checklist. Just before I left MDA, I sold a large project in Asia for receiving pictures from the LANDSAT satellites as well as from weather satellites. About 15 months later, about the time the project was due to be installed, MDA called me with an urgent plea for help.

The shipment was being held up in customs and, after a three-week delay, the reason was still a mystery. MDA asked me to go overseas and troubleshoot the situation on a consulting basis. For MDA, the situation was desperate, because 40% of the $6.5 million project price was to be paid to MDA when the equipment arrived at the designated site. Time was a big issue because MDA was paying high interest to finance the project, and if the installation deadline passed, heavy penalty payments would rapidly eat up profits. Upon meeting with the customer, I discovered to my surprise that the building to house the station had not been built. Although our customer himself was not at fault, he was embarrassed and had no extra budget to solve the problem. We were all stuck, and for MDA the financial countdown clock was ticking loudly.

My solution was to hire an architect and a contractor to quickly erect a temporary building, just adequate to allow the station to operate. As soon as I awarded these contracts, the customs problem dissolved, the customer came up with a temporary storage facility, and the payment was released. Although it may seem like an easily-solved problem in retrospect, it took me two months to complete this negotiation.

How could this problem have been avoided? When I left MDA, someone should have taken over *the relationship of trust* I had with the customer and our local representative so that the company

> Business, more than any occupation, is a continual dealing with the future; it is a continual calculation, an instinctive exercise in foresight.
> —Henry R. Luce

would have had early warning of the problem. The project manager should have made periodic visits to ensure that the *customer's contributions* to the project were on schedule. This story also shows that, if things go wrong, you *cannot rely on the contract to protect your interests,* no matter how comprehensive it may be. We all learned important lessons from this incident and MDA has continued its rapid growth to dominate the world market in this specialized business.

APPLYING THE WHOLE PRODUCT MODEL

Building the Whole Product Model

Market Pull. If the initial idea for your application came from a well-accepted need in the market and you have designed your Core Product to meet it, then determining the other components of the Whole Product Model should come relatively easily. In this "market pull" situation, most customers in the target market can help in defining the Application and what is required to implement it. Both the sailing school and weather station examples represent this case.

Technology Push. If your technology and the Application you propose are new to a potential market, there is a possibility that many potential customers will not immediately appreciate how it could be of value to them. In 1975, how many people knew they needed personal computers, fax machines, or cellular phones? A typical market survey at the time would probably have come up highly negative for all of these current business staples. In fact, most of the new products that we now take for granted were the result of considerable technology push rather than market pull.

If you are in a technology push situation, it is particularly important to first gain the trust, interest, and help of a small number of customers.

> The winds of change that can lead to a crisis or opportunity are classified as "strategic inflection points."
> —Dr. Andrew Grove, president, Intel

Their cooperation is needed to develop an intensive understanding of your target market and to get their help in developing the Whole Product.

Product and Marketing Strategy

The job of utilizing the Whole Product Model to develop a new product is part of the process of researching and creating a complete marketing strategy. In some companies where this process has been formalized, the product manager is responsible for generating a document known as a market requirements specification, and for making sure it is implemented.

Senior management must be involved in the formulation of the strategy because it defines the business you are in and leads to a significant commitment of resources. The Whole Product Model also serves as a practical guide for costing, pricing, analyzing financial feasibility, and monitoring the business performance of your product.

SUMMARY

I have covered three key themes in this chapter:

1. Relationships. Develop and maintain close relationships with your customers, first to design a successful product and then to earn and maintain their trust, the most important ingredient for long-term business.

2. Customer's Point of View. Look at your product from your customer's point of view and use this perspective as an aid in designing it.

3. Whole Product Model. Organize your thinking by using the Whole Product Model as a checklist, first to capture the information you need and then to ensure your customer gets everything needed to be successful with the product.

BURST INTO ACTION

You can't build a reputation on what you're going to do.

—Henry Ford

1 Ask your customers what they think your competencies, strengths, and weaknesses are.

2 Visit several places where your product is used or might be used. Observe what is happening and ask the people there where your product fits in and how they are involved with it.

3 Ask questions to find out: What is your product part of? What is its purpose? What is the application? What business are you really in?

4 Ask your customers how much it costs them, all things considered, to implement the application.

5 To find out how your customers value your product, ask them: What is important to them about the application and the part your product plays in it?

6 To clarify a value and understand their evidence criteria, ask customers: How will you know when you have it? How, exactly, do you measure it?

7 Determine who your customers are. Identify all the organizations and people involved. What does the product mean to each of them and how do they value it?

8 Define the product by filling in the nine components of the product model, considering your customer's viewpoint in all cases. What will be your costs to deliver or ensure provision of each?

9 Determine how each of the components is supplied now, and by whom? How might that change?

10 What opportunities do you now see for making your product more accessible to a wider market? For creating additional value? For changing your promotional approach? For new applications and new markets?

FINDING THE RIGHT CUSTOMERS
From Niches to Riches

Theodore W. Garrison III

Theodore W. Garrison III
works with contractors and
related businesses that want to
grow to the next level. He
works both with individual companies and with trade associations and organizations that want to help their members. His programs focus on sales and marketing, customer service, leadership, and innovation in business.

He has more than 25 years of business, leadership, and motivation experience working in the construction and real estate development industries. He has held executive positions involved with the design, construction and marketing of almost a billion dollars worth of construction, including hotels, office buildings, and public facilities. He has been a licensed real estate broker since 1981. Garrison Associates provides individual counseling as well as seminars and keynote speeches to businesses and associations. His clients include Associated Builders and Contractors, Construction Management Association of America, AT&T, and Skillpath. His talks are both informative and entertaining.

Garrison is a member of the National Speakers Association and the American Seminar Leaders Association. He has contributed chapters to *Marketing for People Not in Marketing, Celebrate Selling,* and *Celebrate Customer Service.*

Theodore W. Garrison III, Garrison Associates, 900 W. Valley Road, Suite 201H, Wayne, PA 19087; phone (610) 341-8605; fax (610) 889-0901; e-mail garrison@bellatlantic.net.

FINDING THE RIGHT CUSTOMERS
From Niches to Riches

Theodore W. Garrison III

There are no non-niche markets anymore.

—Tom Peters

In 1937, Leon Murstein, a young immigrant, started as a cab driver in New York City. He became successful and started buying taxi licenses. When it came time to sell his licenses, he financed them himself, thus starting a company that last year earned almost 50% net margins. Medallion Financial is now a publicly traded company that has lent $700 million to cab drivers based on the collateral of the permit medallion. Medallion says it has never lost a nickel on any of its "taxi" loans.

This is how many niche market successes occur—you develop personal expertise and credentials, then you specialize in working with people like you. You know the area better than your competitors, and the people in the area trust you because you're "one of them."

WHAT IS NICHE MARKETING?

The term *niche marketing* tends to be used interchangeably with *target marketing* or *segmentation*, but it isn't quite the same. A target market or segment is a group of prospects and customers who have similar needs. Niche marketing *can* mean a focus on a particular type of customer, but that definition is from the service or product provider's perspective. From the customer's viewpoint, niche marketing can mean your specialized expertise that you bring to the relationship—why they want to work with you. Doing what you are best at helps you to dominate your business niche.

> ### How to Define a Niche
>
> A niche can be defined by the type of customer you serve, but it can also be defined by:
> - what you offer
> - how you deliver your product or service
> - location, price, quality, speed, customer service
> - or any other unique selling proposition (USP)

Business guru Tom Peters recommends that every business become a specialist. Don Peppers and Martha Rogers, authors of *The One to One Future* and *Enterprise One to One*, take it even further. They encourage marketers "to build dialogues with individual customers." How important is "one to one" marketing? George Gendron of *Inc.* magazine called *The One to One Future* "one of the two or three most important business books ever written."

WHY SHIFT TO NICHE MARKETING?

Successful companies are focusing on smaller and smaller markets. There are many reasons contributing to the shift away from mass marketing. Four of the key developments are discussed below and include: the customer's need for an emotional connection to a product or service, the customer's perception, quality as defined by the customer, and doing it the customer's way. The good news is that each of these challenges can be successfully addressed by switching to a niche marketing approach.

Strong Emotion Is Needed

Professor Robert A. Peterson from the University of Texas says that, despite popular belief, great customer service doesn't generate repeat business unless emotion is added to the equation. In other words, people are only loyal to those products and services that turn them on. And it's a lot easier to feel an emotional connection to a company that specializes in serving you and people just like you. One reason Apple Computer has survived is that many users feel an emotional connection to the Mac computer and against Microsoft. It's no coincidence that Apple was known for taking an "evangelistic" approach to recruiting supporters and software developers. Apple failed as a general platform, but is still very strong in niches like graphic designers.

Customer Perceptions Determine Behavior

In their classic marketing book *Positioning*, Al Ries and Jack Trout emphasized that marketing is essentially a battle for the customer's mind.

Today's customers have a difficult time accepting the idea that mass-marketed products or services are best suited for their needs. In some cases, the difference between a mass-produced versus custom product or service is only in the perception of the customers, but marketers must understand that customers' perceptions are what determine their behavior. For instance, in the newsletter business, a new newsletter marketed

> In whatever you do—whether it's the service you provide or the way you set up your office—make sure there is a 'wow factor,' something that will grab people's attention and make them notice that you've sweated the details.
> —Carl Sewell,
> *Customers for Life*

as the only "membership benefit" of a group usually sells better and has better renewals than the same newsletter without the emotional attachment to a group. When customers feel part of something, their perceptions are different.

Or take trade shows. Niche-oriented trade shows are becoming more popular. Doug Ducate of the Center for Exhibition Industry Research calls this simple customer service. He says "The traditional horizontal trade show, as it gets bigger, can only appeal to the lowest common denominator between attendees." Despite the fact that a bigger show may contain all the same resources as the niche show, plus more, nobody thinks of themselves as a "common denominator." All attendees want a show they can see as just for them.(See also Chapter 9.)

> ## Personalized Consumer Products
>
> Many mass-produced products will no longer be competitive. Consumers are increasingly better informed and harder to please. They want products that satisfy their own tastes rather than accepting whatever stores present.
>
> This market driver will force companies to be even more consumer-driven in designing and marketing products. Understanding consumers' motivations and behavior patterns rather than just their expressed desires is the challenge of consumer product development for the next decade.
>
> —Battelle's Breakthrough Center

Quality Is in the Eye of the Customer

No matter how superior your product or service, unless you address the specific needs of the customer, the customer will not perceive your product as the better product. The collapse of the steel giants in the United States—U.S. Steel and Bethlehem—was not because of high wages and foreign competition. Instead, the steel giants were knocked from their lofty perch by their own arrogance.

The steel giants marketed their steel in a mass-market approach that emphasized volume instead of flexibility for their customers' needs.To maintain volume, they had to produce their products in configurations that were convenient for them and not their customers. Since the product did not meet customers' specific needs, the quality was perceived as poor. While the steel giants were able to provide their products at a slightly lower cost with their mass marketing approach, often customers had additional costs to adapt products to their specific needs.

In this case, the customers were justified in their perceptions that the large mills were not serving their needs. Basically the steel giants told their customers, "We have the best product—take it or leave it." Customers left it. Suddenly the steel giants found their market shrinking.

As the giant steel companies continued to move to larger and larger mills with less and less flexibility, John H. McConnell, founder of Worthington Steel, recognized the opportunity for a niche steel company. Worthington was founded, and operates today, on the philosophy of providing steel to customers the way they want it. In 1955, the steel giants controlled the market, yet McConnell borrowed $600 to run his first steel order. Last fiscal year, Worthington Industries had grown to a $1.6 billion dollar operation. Even more impressive is that fact that during the 1980s Worthington Industries had a higher return on investment than IBM—not bad for company in a battered industry.

> We needed to get cycle times closer to our customers' lead times, so that product could be manufactured based on true customer demand.
>
> —Dave Geib,
> project
> manager,
> Worthington
> Steel

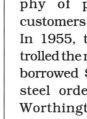

Customers Want It Their Way

Probably the most significant difference between niche marketing and mass marketing is the emphasis on the customer.

The mass-marketing approach has always been to position a product or service and then seek new customers to use that product or service. The problem with this approach is customers' growing resistance to generic products. If a business wants to survive in the 21st century, it will need to adapt its marketing to a customer-oriented approach.

Today's customers demand that products and services be developed specifically for them. This concept has propelled the tremendous success of Dell and Gateway computer companies. Their offer to customize a computer to customers' specific requirements has forced other companies to adopt their approach. Their niche is computer buyers who know enough about computers to specify exactly what they want and can therefore order by phone. Both companies then employ the concept of one-to-one marketing to produce a personally designed computer for their customers.

> The idea of being all things to all people is a thing of the past.
>
> —Michael Dell, chairman and CEO, Dell Computer

The one-to-one concept works even in hamburgers—Burger King had its most successful stretch when it emphasized "Have it your way."

WHY DO COMPANIES NOT WANT TO NICHE MARKET?

Many companies have resisted niche marketing. One simple reason is that it is hard to find or develop a niche. Many companies really don't have a distinguishing philosophy. They are in the "me too" business.

Second, it takes more effort to connect with customers. It takes planning and work to develop better relationships and is less routine. Relationships depend on staff members at every level and are hard to systematize.

The old economy (such as the big steel companies) was based on mass marketing efficiencies. In the past, only the wealthy could afford personally tailored clothing. Mass production raised the quality of off-the-rack clothing. When companies can still make profits without tailoring things for each customer, most will stay with mass marketing. It worked for the big department stores for many years. (Meanwhile, their markets were being eaten away by more "niched" competitors.)

Fear of Loss

Aside from a general lack of focus and vision, perhaps the biggest reason companies don't commit to niche marketing is that they are afraid that they will miss most of their potential buyers. For instance, if you are a consultant, you can probably help a wide range of clients. Likewise for a contractor, doctor, and so forth. While niches can be defined as how you do what you do, this fear is greatest about niches based on target markets. What many people don't realize is that they can serve more than one niche market.

For instance, Medallion Finance *first* specialized in taxi cab financing. They are even named after the "medallion" license of cabs. While that is a very profitable niche for them, they realized that one important factor in their success was that immigrants who bought cabs would do whatever it took to make it in America. So now Medallion also finances dry cleaners and other small businesses run by immigrants. If Medallion is smart in choosing

---

When Less Is More

Some manufacturers use Account Specific Marketing (ASM) with their retailers. It's a type of one-to-one marketing. With ASM, you behave differently with each customer. That's what personal service is all about.

A recent study by the University of Maryland and the National Account Management Association confirms this. Salespeople with *fewer* accounts do better than those with more accounts. Most customers could give you additional business. Focusing your efforts on fewer customers and prospects lets you build relationships, provide better service, get referrals, and so forth. Chasing after everyone makes you ineffective for all.

—Rick Crandall, *1001 Ways to Market Your Services: Even If You Hate to Sell*

credit risks, they can develop niches based on many of the types of businesses they choose to finance.

You can even create different niches based on different price points with similar products or services. To do this, you would probably choose to maintain different product names, just as General Motors had success with Cadillac, Buick, Chevy, and so forth for many years.

THE BENEFITS OF CREATING A NICHE

Knowledge Is the Key

The old mass-marketing approach emphasized product knowledge—meaning the product or service being sold. The mentality was that if you knew the capabilities of your product or service, you could demonstrate how they could be adapted to help your customer.

In today's marketplace, customers demand more from providers than just expertise on their products and services. Customers are demanding ever increasing knowledge about their businesses. This is a fundamental reason for the shift to niche marketing.

Expertise about your customers is not about collecting data on your customers. Many mass marketers have all kinds of data about their customers. Usually this data is demographic in nature and really does not help the provider understand customers' problems. Effective marketing requires that you learn how your customers operate and understand the challenges they face from their perspectives. To do this, you must become an expert in your customers' industries, if not their businesses.

Who has time for this, you ask. You do, if you want to succeed in the 21st century!

> We are in the midst of a revolution . . . those organizations and individuals who can create new relationships with customers will find themselves with unimagined competitive advantage. Those who don't will lose.
> —Larry Wilson,
> *Stop Selling,
> Start Partnering*

Customize

Obviously, it is impossible to become an expert in every industry. Instead, marketers need to combine products or services with their expertise in a particular industry or industry segment.

For example, an attorney with a small legal practice might decide to hire an accounting firm to handle all the firm's bookkeeping functions. Two firms apply for the job. The first accounting firm provides services to all kinds of small businesses. They use a small-business software package that is adequate for most small businesses.

The second firm specializes in providing accounting services for lawyers. The principal of this firm was an office manager for a large legal firm and understands the special accounting requirements of the legal profession. Their software program is designed for attorneys and all the special accounting issues of the legal profession. Which firm would you hire? Probably the legal specialist. Even if they were more expensive? Most likely.

Building an Industry Presence

Accountant Chris Frederiksen had one credit union as a client. He asked their trade group for information on niche-specific tax issues. That led to a referral to a second job. He began to speak publicly for the association. (He was the only accountant who'd ever shown that much interest in their problems.) Eventually, he had more credit union clients than any other accountancy firm in California.

The fact that the second accountant charges a little more doesn't really matter, because he will handle the attorney's practice more efficiently in the long run and therefore will actually cost less when all expenses are considered. The attorney is not producing billable time when she is working with her accountant, so she must keep this time to a minimum. Since the second accountant charges a little bit more, he had increased his profit margins, but his overall efficiency will reduce the attorney's overall costs. It is a true win-win situation.

Specialize

Developing customer expertise gives you the information you need to modify your products and services to fit your customer's needs. Obviously, every customer will have its own special problems, but the more carefully a niche is defined, the greater the common ground that will exist from customer to customer. As you begin to understand each customer's individual needs, you begin to move into one-to-one marketing—the ultimate niche market.

In the construction industry for example, even the largest contractors specialize. *Engineering News-Record* magazine reports that nine of the 10 largest contractors derived at least 51% of their work from one classification of construction, such as industrial/petrochemical or highways. One contractor obtained 98% of its income from a single classification and another, 100% from a single classification.

> Specialization, specialization.
> You'll rule the barnyard,
> If you specialize.
>
> —Marilyn Monroe in the 1960 movie, *Let's Make Love*

The point here is that if the biggest companies with their large volumes can be successful by specializing, the opportunities are even greater for smaller companies. Smaller companies do not have the resources to establish their customer expertise in many areas. With niche marketing, they can be a big expert in a small niche. The fewer resources you have, the more restricted your niche should be, because it will require fewer resources to establish your position.

YOUR COMPETITIVE POSITION

Even if a niche didn't allow you to do a better job for customers, most customers would prefer to deal with a specialist. They don't want to have to invest in training you!

In the construction industry, the difference between a petrochemical plant and a highway is clear. However, many contractors express frustration over the fact that prospects want to divide the construction of buildings into narrower niches such as hotels, high-rise office buildings, manufacturing plants, retail operations, and others. Note that in this case, customers are clamoring for niche service.

Customers Want Specialists

Building owners often are reluctant to hire contractors to build a type of building the contractor has never built before. The contractors honestly believe they can build any type of building—after all, buildings are buildings and it should not make a difference what the building is used for. Having been a contractor, I tend to sympathize with the contractors' view. However, having spent many years representing building owners, I must disagree with these contractors.

I would be the first to acknowledge that a competent contractor could probably build any type of building. But my experience has taught me that contractors who are familiar with a particular type of building bring more to the partnership. They know where to obtain specialized supplies and subcontractors. They are better able to anticipate problems. They speak the "language" of that type of building, and it takes less effort on the part of the building owner to coordinate the contractor's work. This is a direct result of the contractor's increased experience with this type of building.

Narrow Your Niche

It's common for marketers to not define their niches narrowly enough. For instance, the online Dental Zone (www.saveyoursmile.com) could be considered a niche (people who are interested in dental issues online).

But the site creators found that by *really* specializing they became more important to clients, and much more attractive to advertisers. They created the Canker Sore Relief Center, the Healthy Gum Center, the Parents Guide to Children's Dentisty area, and so forth. Those were tight niches and attracted much more interest.

The experienced contractor knows what is required and expected and can anticipate potential issues unique to a particular type of building.

Increased Customer Loyalty

An experienced contractor is more valuable to the building owner, which results in greater customer loyalty. This is a perfect example of understanding what the customer needs versus understanding your product or service.

If a contractor has never built a hospital for example, they would not be able to advise the owner of possible problems unique to the construction of hospitals or deal as effectively with the many unique hospital construction-related issues. Without this experience, owners would be forced to uncover these issues themselves. It is not a matter of the contractor's construction expertise, but a matter of the contractor's knowledge of the customer's unique needs.

> ### Working a Niche
>
> An attorney specialized in legal issues for one type of construction subcontractor. He now works for half of the companies in his area. His business boomed because of referrals (which happens when you specialize). When he gets all the possible business from this specialty, he'll gradually add another. After all, his clients work with lots of other contractors.

Another example of having the expertise the client wants is the speaking industry. Consider the case of a speaker who is an expert on marketing. A marketing expert will be able to apply the general principles to any industry. But, speakers and trainers who are experts in their industries can bring real-life experiences to their audiences.

General principles are fine, but success is all in the implementation. For example, the marketing expert might talk about the importance of repeat business. But hearing generalities doesn't give the audience a clear path to implementation. The specifics of how a fast food restaurant motivates its customers to return are different than how lawyers motivate their clients to use their services again.

The last two examples emphasize the importance of learning about the customer. This requirement is becoming more and more critical because customers are demanding it. When you develop a niche in the customer's industry, you know each customers' problems better and can help them more easily and effectively.

SUMMARY: HOW TO CARVE OUT YOUR NICHE

To develop a niche, it is necessary to gain a superior knowledge of your customers' businesses. This knowledge will give you a better understanding of how your products and services are used within your customers' operations. Here are five ways to build a niche:

1 **Emphasize your experience.** For example, the accountant who had worked for a law firm would emphasize his experience in handling issues unique to law firms. A contractor would emphasize the successful completion of similar projects.

However, even with experience, you can't sit back. You need to employ some of the other niche builders listed below. The world keeps changing and to remain an expert you can never stop learning.

2 **Work with your current customers to increase your knowledge of their needs.** Improving your relationships with current customers is an ongoing process. If you have good products or services, you should already have credibility within your marketing niche. The idea here is to use your knowledge to help your customers im-

> In the business world, everyone is paid in two coins: cash and experience. Take the experience first; the cash will come later.
> —Harold Geneen, ITT

prove their businesses. This will change your status from a mere vendor to that of a consultant or even a partner. Often, you will have one or two good customers who can lead you into a new niche. If you've taken good care of them, they will help you gain business with other people like them. This is often how new niches are developed.

3 **If you are new in business or want to venture into a new niche where you don't have any experience, don't give up.** You merely need to do your homework. Start by learning everything you can about the niche you are interested in. Read their trade magazines. Join their trade associations. Attend their conventions. In essence, become one of them.

4 **Look for opportunities to speak before the members of your niche, especially the decision makers.** For example, if you provide environmental consulting services to the pesticide industry, you might speak at their trade association meetings and update them on changes in the environmental regulations that affect them. This doesn't mean you give a sales pitch for your services. Instead, you provide information of value to your niche members. In this way, you demonstrate your expertise and build your credibility.

Create Your Niche

You can't afford to wait for business to come to you. Digital Prepress decided to focus on the select market of real estate agents who wanted professional-looking promotion sheets customized for each house or broker. By finding and creating niche markets, Digital gets business while other printers sit and wait.

---

5 **Write articles for the publications that your niche customers read.** Again, these will not be a sales pitch for your services (they wouldn't get published if they were!). Published articles build your reputation and establish your knowledge. Get an article published (even if you have to use a ghost writer) and you become a "recognized expert."

IN CONCLUSION

Niche marketing allows you to leverage your expert status within your niche. This leads to greater credibility and increased word-of-mouth referrals.

In the 1970s, when someone needed a computer, advice from peers was often something similar to, "Nobody ever got fired for buying an IBM." You want to be the "safe" option for your niche members.

The idea is to develop a relationship with your customers somewhere between a consultant and a partner. The closer you can get to the elite partner status, the more entrenched you will become. Once you reach this status, price will no longer be the controlling factor, which allows you the opportunity to increase your profit margins.

Commit now to finding your niche or creating your niche, then nail it!

BURST INTO ACTION

Yesterday is a canceled check; tomorrow is a promissory note; today is ready cash—use it.

—John D. Rockefeller

1 List the kinds of niches you serve.
2 List the things you do that are different from others in your industry.
3 List several ways to make your customers feel like they belong to a distinct group (for example, a buyers club, offering member-only events).
4 Find out what quality means from your customers' perspective.
5 List ways you can develop one-to-one relationships with each customer.
6 List ways you can build emotional connections with your customers.

7 Develop specific sales pieces or resumes for each niche you serve.

8 Collect testimonials that are specific to each niche in which you work.

9 Develop a list of where you can speak or write for your niches.

TEN STEPS TO RAPPORT
How to Become the Emotional Twin of Your Prospect

Ray Leone

Ray Leone
began in the field of computer science as consultant for First Pennsylvania Bank, RCA, and UNIVAC. He left that field to enter sales, becoming a top ten producer for two international corporations. Combining his scientific background with his practical field experience, Mr. Leone developed his Sales Funnel™ selling system. Thousands of salesmasters around the world have been "funneled."

Corporations that have retained Mr. Leone as a consultant include AT&T, EDS, Lucent Technologies, Greentree Financial, Wachovia, Atlanta Journal, Sprint, Clemson University, Canteen Vending, Scansource, Prudential, Tempnet, Teledyne Laars, and The Compass Group.

Mr. Leone is the author of the best-selling book *Success Secrets of the Sales Funnel,* and is host of the radio show "Winning the Game of Life."

As a businessmen, Mr. Leone is president of The Leone Resource Group and SSS Publishing. He is a member of the National Speakers Association, American Management Association, and the American Society for Training and Development.

Ray Leone, Leone Resource Group, Box 16039, Charleston, SC 29412; phone (843) 795-9462; e-mail rleone@tpn.com; Internet www.rayleone.com.

10 STEPS TO RAPPORT
How to Become the Emotional Twin of Your Prospect

Ray Leone

> All things being equal, people buy from people they like. All things not being so equal, people still buy from people they like."
>
> —Mark McCormack, *What They Don't Teach You at Harvard Business School*

We can make our prospects feel comfortable by becoming more like them in as many ways as possible—in effect becoming their emotional twin. This builds rapport, the key ingredient to successful selling and communicating. It is important to note that this is not something you do *to* people; it is something you do *for* them.

The more alike we are, the fewer the barriers to communication. Clear communication of the message leads to a win-win relationship.

This includes nonverbal communication which can account for the majority of people's impressions of us.

Based on misreporting of the studies by psychologist Albert Mehrabian, many popular authors and speakers claim that only 7% of our communication is in what we say, with 38% in tone and pace, and 55% in body language.

In fact, the emphasis on each channel depends on the circumstances and the person. However, the best current estimate is that, on average, about 35% of communication is based on what we say, and the rest on nonverbal factors.

DO THEY HEAR WHAT YOU MEAN?

During research for a speech I was preparing for a college fraternity, I asked the Director of Global Business Development for EDS, Tom Metz, what he thought was the most important principle for effective communication that I should share with these young adults. He advised, "Make sure they always receive confirmation of what they thought has been communicated—both as a sender and as a receiver."

Is it possible to misinterpret a conversation? Yes, it happens all the time.

Stephen Covey, in his book, *The 7 Habits of Highly Effective People,* explains how your beliefs and past experiences affect the way you interpret messages or events. Your paradigm is the lens through which you look at the world. For example, a white southerner whose grandfather died in the Civil War has a different definition of the Confederate flag than does a black American whose grandfather was a slave.

The more we mesh with another person's beliefs, paradigms, actions, and personality, the greater the rapport. The greater the rapport, the greater the likelihood of a doing business together.

You may be thinking, "Great Ray, I believe you. But how do we become people's emotional twins, especially if we have never met them before?"

I am glad you asked. Here are the ten ingredients to developing rapport:

> Our paradigms are "the way we 'see' the world—not in terms of our visual sense of sight, but in terms of perceiving, understanding, interpreting."
> —Stephen Covey, *The 7 Habits of Highly Effective People*

1 Personality profiles.

Many systems distinguish four dominant personality profiles. The Myers Briggs and DISC™ are the two most popular personality profiling instruments.

I find the DISC™ system easier to remember and apply to daily life. Personality differences are the basis of human behavior from which grow all other applications including how to sell, how to communicate, how to motivate, and how to manage. Using the DISC™ system, you identify personality profiles of individuals by the characteristics they display (see chart below).

Of course, most of us use different styles in different situations. Many of us also may combine two or more of the styles.

If you give a presentation without regard to personality differences, you will miss the mark 75% of the time! (For more information on DISC™ and its applications, please contact me.)

> Because people are different and need different treatment, use the "Platinum Rule®" not the Golden Rule. Treat them the way THEY want to be treated. There is nothing more unequal than the equal treatment of unequals.
> —Ken Blanchard

DISC™ Profiles

Dominant (D)
- Dominant
- Decision maker
- Do it now
- Results-oriented
- Impatient
- Appears insensitive
- Resists personal criticism

Interactive (I)
- Life of party
- Enthusiastic
- Do it now
- Disorganized
- Hates details
- Loves challenge
- Good verbal skills

Steadfast (S)
- Team player
- Security-minded
- Resist sudden change
- Family-oriented
- Does things later

Cautious (C)
- Do it later
- Reserved
- Critical thinker
- Conscientious
- Accurate

2 **Primary sensory mode.** All of us process information through a primary sensory mode—either *auditory, visual* or *kinesthetic.* If we present—communicate—in our prospect's dominant mode, they receive more of the message.

Conversely, when we communicate in a different mode than our prospect, then he or she is missing much of the message. For example, if you process information visually and I give a verbal presentation without visual aids, then I am not being as effective as I might.

If I were selling a car to a kinesthetic person, I would say, "Feel the leather. Notice how the seats hug your body, just like the car hugs the road."

To a visual, I would say, "Picture yourself driving down the road and the reaction of your friends when they see you in this car."

To an auditory, I would say, "Listen to the solid sound the door makes when you close it. The stereo wraps the music around you . . ." You get the idea.

The clues to sensory mode are eye movement, rate of speech, and vocabulary.

Ask someone to remember their best sale or happiest day and watch their eyes.

Visuals look up to the right or left when trying to recall (picture) something. They generally speak fast and use phrases like, "I see what you mean."

Auditories look sideways when recalling information. Their speech is moderate and even. They use phrases like, "I hear what you are saying."

Tune In

Once identified, tune your communication style into the customer or prospect's station:

TO THE DOMINANT RECEIVER
- Be brief and to the point.
- Display confidence.
- Defend your position.

TO THE INTERACTIVE RECEIVER
- Minimize details.
- Be friendly and demonstrative.
- Emphasize the positive.
- Allow for interruption.

TO THE STEADFAST RECEIVER
- Be slow and steady.
- Be truthful and sincere.

TO THE CAUTIOUS RECEIVER
- Respect their space.
- Be specific and use facts.
- Do not get personal.

Presentation Tip: Start Multimodal

When presenting to a group or someone whose sensory mode is unknown to you, give a multisensory presentation. Use some visual, auditory, and kinesthetic cues and see how they respond.

Kinesthetics look down when recalling an event. Their speech is slow and deliberate. They use phrases like, "I feel I understand what you are saying."

3 **Rate, pace, and tone.** When I ask what Northerners think when they hear a Southerner speak, they reply that their first impressions are that Southerners are slow and stupid. When I ask Southerners what they think when they hear a Northerner speak, Southerners report that they perceive Northerners as shifty, pushy, and uncouth. What are these reactions based on? Rate of speech.

If you are an individual with a Northern accent selling to someone in the South, or vice versa, imagine how difficult it is to get past the perceptions.

To maximize the effectiveness of your communication, match the tone, pace, and rate of speech of your prospect. Notice how network news anchors are moderate in their pitch and tone. That is because they must appeal to a broad segment of the population and, more importantly, not alienate anyone because of their delivery.

4 **Life control.** I was very fortunate during the late 1970s to have sold a big-ticket item to Sheldon Glass, a prominent psychiatrist, educator, and author of the book *Life-Control.*

Not long after I met him, Dr. Glass gave me a copy of his book. I read it and was struck immediately by its relevance to selling, life, relationships—everything. Dr. Glass's theory was not designed specifically to relate to selling, but it is a perfect match. His theory is that every time we encounter

I've found that every group (and its leaders and members) goes through an identifiable cycle, beginning with the moment it considers taking on a task to the time the goal is achieved.

—Sheldon Glass,
Life-Control

new ideas, experiences, or challenges, we go through four distinct phases.

Introductory phase. Dr. Glass: "This is a period during which new goals are worked out and agreed upon. This is a time of excitement, even euphoria. Interesting, promising new things are about to happen."

It is when Ray and Linda are first considering buying that new home.

Resistance-testing phase. Dr. Glass: "This is when the group reacts with anxiety to the change that the new goals require. It both resists that change and tests the leadership to see if it can handle the process. This is a time of uncertainty, disagreement, and general travail. The status quo has been shattered and replaced by something less comfortable."

Using the previous analogy, Ray and Linda experience concerns about moving to a new neighborhood and having to pay high interest rates. This phase if often marked by adjustments, conflicts, and arguments. In the buying cycle, it manifests itself as objections.

Productive phase. Dr. Glass: "This is when the group works to accomplish the task and meaningful change takes place. It's when the arguments subside and goal-directed work begins in earnest."

This is the "get-down-to-business" stage, when concerns and objections are resolved by Ray and Linda and they move toward the purchase of that new home.

Termination phase. Dr. Glass: "This is when the goal is accomplished, the group consolidates its knowledge, and the cycle comes to an end."

The cycle for Ray and Linda would end with the purchase of the home.

Not every member of a group may be in the same phase at the same time. This is the cause of most conflicts and disagreements. Ray may be ready to buy that new house, while Linda hasn't accepted the idea of moving to a new neighborhood.

There are many variations and angles to Dr. Glass's theory. Most of all, it helps you understand why people do what they do, especially as you learn to recognize and understand these patterns.

A Car-buying Example

Here's another example of applying the cycle model. As mentioned, the cycle can be applied to virtually any experience or progression in life, from buying a car to planning a vacation. Let me give a quick example of how simple the application of this theory can be. Suppose you and your spouse consider buying a new car. Let me break the typical scenario into components:

Introductory phase. You say, "We need a new car. Let's go look at them tonight." Your spouse says "Great! It will be fun."

Resistance-testing phase. After seeing various cars, a discussion ensues about trade-in value and having to pay the sales tax that dampens your enthusiasm. You even have difficulty deciding on a car both of you want.

Productive phase. After a short time, you not only come to grips (a kinesthetic phrase) with the sales tax and trade-in issue, but you also agree on a price range and make.

Termination phase. With all plans ironed out, you and your spouse go to the dealership that offers the vehicle you want.

The important point is to determine what phase your prospects are in when they appear before you. They could be in any of the four phases. You must recognize their phase and get in-phase with them before you can lead them along the road to rapport.

5 **Matching buying strategy.** We all do things for one of two reasons—a desire for pleasure or the avoidance of pain.

In my seminars when I say avoidance of pain is the stronger motivator, it creates lively discussion. I prove it by asking, "Isn't it true that if you own your own business, you have the potential to make more money than if you work for someone else?" Everyone agrees. "Then why doesn't everyone work for themselves?" Ah! Because the potential to fail and the risk of pain are greater.

Features and Benefits

Traditional sales presentations use features/benefits statements where the salesperson describes a feature and then bridges to the benefit with the phrase, "Which means to you ..."

Example: Feature: Air bags in our cars. Benefit: Reduced chance of injury in the event of an accident.

Feature/benefit statement: "We equip all of our cars with air bags, which means to you, in the event of an accident, your chances of injury are greatly reduced."

Pain Avoidance

That is fine for those people who buy for the benefit a product delivers. However, a large segment, maybe the majority of people, buy to avoid negatives.

You can determine their buying strategy by asking, "Mrs. Prospect, what will owning this copier mean to you?"

If she says, "It will give us increased capability. Our promotional brochures will have greater impact and we will be able to accomplish more in less time," then she is a person who buys for the benefits, also known as a move-toward person.

If she says, "I'm tired of the old copier always breaking down and my secretary complaining about how messy it is to change toner," then she is a person who buys to avoid pain, also known as a move-away person.

Everyone knows how to give a move-toward, feature-benefit presentation. To increase your sales success, learn to give a move-away presentation by emphasizing what they will lose by not buying.

A technique we use in our Sales Funnel™ system (described in my book *Success Secrets of the Sales Funnel*) is to create pain or discomfort in our prospect, and then provide the aspirin (the solution) that removes the pain.

Fifty percent of my income is the result of using this technique when sitting in the first-class section on an airplane. I will ask the CEO sitting next to me a series of questions that make her feel uncomfortable with her management team.

I'll ask a question like, "In terms of college semesters, how many semesters of leadership training, not management training, has your leadership team had?" The answer most often is "none." Then I say, "You wouldn't have a doctor without a medical degree, or an attorney without a law degree. Then why have a leadership team be in positions of responsibility where they have had no training for the job?" Big-time pain and deficit!

Match your message to the buying strategy of your prospects and watch your sales soar.

6 **Trust and credibility.** Before someone will listen to you, they must believe that you know what you are talking about. Are you credible? And they must believe that you care about them.

> No one cares how much you know until they know how much you care.
> —Ken Blanchard,
> *The One Minute Manager*

Notre Dame football coach Lou Holtz says there are three questions that must be answered affirmatively before anyone will follow you. They are:

- Can I trust you?
- Do you care about me?
- Are you committed to the goal?

Your prospects must believe these things about you if they are to make a decision based on what you say. To develop rapport with an audience of one or one thousand, they must know that you care and have earned the right to be called a professional salesperson.

As a speaker, I am proudest of the fact that my audiences think that I am from their industry. Whether it's bankers, insurance agents, car dealers, credit union managers, or national franchisees, they know that I care enough to have researched the problems and issues that are specific to them.

The confidence that comes with preparation cannot be achieved in any other way. Your prospects will know that you have earned the right to be there and will respond accordingly.

7 **Body language.** Remember, much of your in-person communication is body language. When you are in an airport, do you form opinions about the people around you—about whether they are successful, happy, sad, confident, or intelligent? I do. And it is all based on body language.

When I owned a swimming pool company, I videotaped myself giving an actual sales presentation in a customer's home. What I learned about body language and myself was startling.

Here is what I saw on the video that I missed during the presentation. The husband leaned back on his chair whenever he got nervous. He was most receptive when we were both leaning forward. The husband and wife exchanged furtive glances while I was busy writing. They picked up the drawing of the pool which indicated to me that they had taken mental possession. Whenever we talked about fishing (the husband's favorite sport), his eyes would widen, he would lean forward and his body would relax. Whenever we talked about price, he would sit straight and constrain his movements. It was obvious that they wanted the pool.

By the way, I learned that I had a terrible habit of twirling my mustache. I looked like the villain in a silent movie. I wonder how many sales that habit cost me.

8 Questions. If you help raise someone's self-esteem, you will increase rapport with that person. Asking questions that uncover the true issues and concerns of prospects, allowing them to do most of the talking, raises their self-esteem.

By asking those questions, you are telling the customers that you care about what they think and feel, further increasing the bond (rapport) between you and them. (See also Chapter 5.)

Ask Great Questions

I've compiled a list that will help you formulate good questions. When you develop a question, test it against my list. The more yes's you get, the more likely it is to be a great question.

- Does the question lower the comfort level of the client?
- Does it uncover pain?
- Does it invite the client to consider new information?
- Does the question focus on an idea that the client has not considered before?

- Does the question require careful thought before the client can formulate a response?
- Does the question increase your credibility?
- Does it reduce your competitor's credibility?
- Does the question move you further down the Sales Funnel™?

When selling swimming pools at an average price of over $20,000, I developed a powerful question that helped me earn over $1,000,000 in commissions. If I were coming to your home to sell you a pool, I would accompany you into the backyard and ask the following question, "Where have you decided to put your primary and secondary focal points?"

Test this question against my list. What happened to my credibility? What happened to my competitor's credibility when they did not ask that question? What happened to your belief that you knew everything you needed to know to make an intelligent decision? Did we create discomfort?

Create a list of several questions that have this impact and watch how differently (a visual phrase) your customers respond to you. You will position yourself as a problem solver, not a salesperson. Your customers will then treat you as a valued resource and not an adversary.

Key Questions

Here is a basic presentation based on just six questions that will lead you to a sale.

1. "Do you know we are the best or do I have to prove it to you?" This question establishes the tone for the entire presentation.

2. "What criteria are you going to use to choose a vendor?" (What is important to you?) Whatever criteria they select leads you to the next question. For example, if they say quality is their main criterion, then question 3 is . . .

3. "What is your definition of quality?" It is presumptuous of us to think that our definition of quality is the same as someone else's. We must make sure that we are addressing their criteria as they define them.

4. "Why is that important to you?" The answer to this question uncovers their dominant buying motive (DBM) or hot button. People buy on emotion and justify with logic. Too many presentations overlook the emotional side of the process.

5. "If I can meet the criteria you stated were important to you, will I be your vendor?"

When dealing with people, remember you are not dealing with creatures of logic, but with creatures of emotions— creatures bristling with prejudice, and motivated by pride and vanity.

—Dale Carnegie

General Guidelines for Becoming a Sales Funnel™ Salesmaster

- The personality profile of the customer determines your strategy and demeanor.
- Ask for commitment prior to the presentation.
- Give the customer the right to disagree.
- Agreement must be obtained on every issue that you consider important or you must not continue down the Funnel.
- Ask questions that create a deficit in the comfort level of the customer.
- The WITY [What's Important To You] is a document that lists buying criteria, product features, and buying motives.

We have asked the customer to buy prior to the presentation. *This is one of the true secrets to sales success.*

Between questions 5 and 6, give your presentation based on the answers and then you are ready for the final question.

6. "What else do you need to know to be convinced that you have found the right ____ ?" (Fill in the blank with the appropriate appendage: builder, vacuum cleaner, car, banker, widget, etc.)

This is the perfect closing question because it can be answered in only two ways. One possible answer is nothing, which means they have bought. The other answer is a request for more information, which gives you permission to continue selling. Not wanting your product is not one of the answers.

9 **Balanced listening.** In Step 8, we asked the questions. In Step 9, we listen to the answers.

Have you ever been introduced to someone and ten seconds later forgotten his or her name? Why?

You weren't listening. Hearing and listening are not the same thing.

Isn't your best friend the one who listens to you without judgment? When we actively listen to prospects, we are telling them that what they say is important to us. When we take notes, that further underscores that we care about what they say.

A number of years ago, an auto manufacturer did an exit survey of people who did not buy a car. The number one reason given for not buying was,

"The salespeople did not listen to me. They gave their favorite presentation, not the one I wanted to hear."

Have you ever been thinking about what you were going to say while someone was talking to you? That is called a two-person monologue.

We can process between 800 and 1200 words per minute and speak at less than 200 words per minute. That leaves an enormous amount of idle time for our minds to occupy. Quite often, we use that time to daydream. Active listening requires a concentrated effort, but like most things, the result is worth the effort.

Just as we have different sensory modes and different personalities, we have different listening styles. Some of us listen more for facts, others listen more for the feelings behind the words.

Your goal should be to balance your listening style between fact and feelings so as to eliminate filters. There is a listening-style profile system put out by the Carlson Learning Company, similar to the DISC™ system, that identifies your listening style. The more we listen to the whole message being sent (verbal and non-verbal), the greater our understanding of our prospect and the greater the rapport.

10 **Adaptability.** Here's where you pull it all together. Once you can use the first nine variables of rapport, you are ready to become the emotional twin of any prospect. Because you can vary your style to match the person, others will be more comfortable with you.

When I first implemented this system, my confidence level soared. I was in total control of the process. I recall the CEO of a $6 billion corporation granting me a 15-minute appointment. Because I established true rapport, the appointment lasted two hours. He was enjoying himself and didn't want to end our conversation.

A leader who possesses the skill of adaptability is heaven sent.
—Sun Tzu, *The Art of War*

AN EXAMPLE

The most dramatic example of the power of rapport occurred when I was giving a presentation to the senior officers of a major financial institution. The CEO was a "High D," visual, move-toward person. The CFO was a "High C," move away-from, auditory person. The Vice President of Sales & Marketing was a "High I," visual, move-toward person. By changing my delivery, pace, style, and body language when addressing each of them, I was able to maximize the effectiveness of the presentation and control the entire process.

For the CEO, I summarized key points and gave them to him in rapid fashion. I arranged to meet with the CFO one hour early because I knew that he would want to go over every detail. I praised him on his ability to uncover ambiguities. I pointed out how our system would prevent mistakes. I gave him reports to substantiate our conclusions. For the VP of Sales, I joked with her and described how other institutions would envy the marketing plan that would support the new services.

Because I adapted to each person and presented the way they preferred, the deal went through. It is still one of the biggest deals of my career.

SUMMARY

Learning to use the techniques discussed will do two things for you. First, it will make you more comfortable because you have a way to read people and adapt to each situation. You have a system to apply. Second, you will make others more comfortable with you. When they are comfortable, they will be more open to your message of how you can help them.

BURST INTO ACTION

It's not where you start, it's where you go.

—Zig Ziglar

1 Adjust your approach to match the personalties of your prospects and to put them at ease.

2 Present in your prospects' primary sensory modes. Convey your message the way they prefer.

3 Match your rate and tone of speech with theirs.

4 Ask questions that elicit their strategies. Understand what they want.

5 Mirror their body language and observe what their body is saying. Become "literate" non-verbally.

6 Be aware that different people can be in different stages of the buying cycle. Bring all parties into the same phase of the buying cycle.

7 Establish trust and credibility by being totally prepared. Do your homework about their industry and situation.

8 Your questions show that you are a professional. Ask questions that let the prospects know that you are there to solve their problem and want to do the best possible job for them.

9 Actively listen. Eliminate your natural filters by balancing your listening between fact and feeling.

10 Take what you have learned in steps 1 through 9 and adjust your presentation and delivery to best match your prospect in every way. Become your prospect's emotional twin and everyone wins.

Good luck and good selling!

ASKING POWERFUL QUESTIONS IS THE KEY TO YOUR SUCCESS

David Klaybor

David Klaybor, ATP, provides companies and entrepreneurs with marketing advice and tips that immediately increase sales. Klaybor researches both corporate and home-based businesses, analyzes their problems, and provides innovative solutions.

Mr. Klaybor gained his experience as an airline captain, real estate broker, business owner, radio talk show co-host, and personal development instructor. He has been teaching for two decades and prides himself on creating "learning systems" that produce measurable results for his clients.

Mr. Klaybor's teaching technologies have earned him feature and cover story articles in major magazines. He has given thousands of wealth-building seminars worldwide to his direct sales and network marketing clients: Fuller Brush, Excel, Prepaid Legal, Rexall, Avon, Amway, Shaklee, Enrich, Quorum, Alliance, LifePlus, FreeLife, and hundreds more. Mr. Klaybor is the author of *Books Don't Work Unless You Do* and *The 4 Secrets to Developing Solid Relationships*. He is the creator of a customized Time Management Business Planner System for Salespeople. He is the author of several audiotapes, and has published his own magazine.

David Klaybor, 1223 Marquette Avenue, South Milwaukee, WI 53172; voicemail (949) 450-3123, (714) 433-2128, or (414) 762-9259; e-mail DKLAYBOR@hotmail.com

ASKING POWERFUL QUESTIONS IS THE KEY TO YOUR SUCCESS

David Klaybor

> Good questioning skills will do more to help you in sales than any "sales techniques" ever could.
>
> —Neil Rackham, *SPIN Selling*

P icture this. You're the owner of a small business. A salesperson comes in the door. "Hi. I'm Bill. I represent ABC Payroll Services. If you have employees, let ABC handle your payroll. We're reasonably priced, reliable, and we'll save you time. Is this something you would be interested in?"

Whew! Did you have time to digest all that? Probably not. You probably would say you're not interested, even though you hate doing payroll.

Now consider this scenario.

MARCY: Hi. I'm Marcy. I help small businesses handle their payroll. Do you have employees?

YOU: *(guardedly)* Yes.

MARCY: I know you must have a lot of things to do—is *now* an OK time to talk.

YOU: *(still guardedly)* For a few minutes.

MARCY: I've noticed your business as I've driven by. You've been here for a while—you must be doing pretty well.

YOU: I'm doing OK. I really need to spend more time marketing though.

MARCY: Do you prepare your own payroll?

YOU: Yes.

MARCY: Is this something you enjoy doing?

YOU: *(with a little laugh)* No. It has to get done, so I do it. But it's hard keeping up on all the regulations. And the end-of-year reports are a real hassle.

MARCY: Have you considered having someone take over this chore for you?

YOU: I figured it's probably too expensive.

Let's stop the conversation here and consider what's happened so far. Marcy has told you very little about her business other than the basic service she provides. But look at what she has learned. She's learned basic qualifying information—that you have employees and do your own payroll. She's discovered that you don't like doing payroll, that you have more important work to do (marketing), that you find payroll regulations confusing, and that you think payroll services are expensive.

Marcy asked questions—and listened to your answers—to uncover your problems and needs. Is this information Marcy can use when she presents the benefits of using ABC Payroll Services? You bet!

Listening for Sales

According to Lucette Comer at Purdue University, research showed that sales reps with higher listening skills were better in all six phases of the sales process: approach, need for identification, presentation, overcoming objections, closing, and after-sales support.

—*What's Working in Sales Management*

ASK THE BEST QUESTIONS FOR WIN/WIN MARKETING

Have you ever wondered why some people earn only the minimum, while others earn $5,000 to $50,000 or more each month? One of the main reasons is a person's ability to uncover, discover, and find out what each prospect needs in order to buy. Successful people do this by communicating with their clients more effectively than do other (less productive) people.

Good Communication Is Not a "Gift of Gab"

> Talk is cheap. Supply exceeds demand.
> —John Fogg

In the sales or "sharing" environment, most people talk endlessly about their businesses. This is a *huge* mistake. Your customers and potential clients do not want to hear you go on and on about how great you are, how great your company or product is, or how miserable their life is without your help.

One-way communication is preaching—it is using declarative statements. Leaders do not "brain dump" everything they know about their companies onto their prospects, hoping that something they say will get through. Instead, superstars, through their masterful use of questions, find out what their clients need and then offer solutions. They use questions to create a two-way, interactive communication cycle.

> The older I grow, the more I listen to people who don't talk much.
> —Henry Ward Beecher

Questions Provide the Pathway to Closing

Asking questions will dramatically improve your business. Here's why: Every time a person asks us something, we have to rethink a thought we've already processed before. That means we have to internalize the matter and choose what action to take—this is how we will decide how to respond to the question. This process is what makes or breaks a marketing encounter.

Every time you ask your prospects or customers a meaningful question, their minds have to review what you have said before they respond. Using questions helps insure that the other person is listening to you and that the person understands the point you are attempting to communicate. Asking questions lets you control the conversation—and the other person is usually happy to have you do it because they get to talk.

Questions Unlock Secrets

For a person striving to become an effective marketer, the most important goal is to ask a series of questions that will get your prospect to tell you everything you need to know to "complete a business transaction" with them. Questions let you qualify people, do a needs analysis, and guide a sales presentation—all at the same time.

Questions do several valuable things:
- They check on the other person's understanding of what you said.
- They make you listen more and prevent your making rambling sales pitches.
- They provide the information you need.
- They give your prospects ownership of their decisions.

If I ask you to choose between several alternatives, when you give me your decision, who's idea is it now? Yours, of course. When you use the questioning process, you are not trying to sell anyone something; you're just asking what they want so you can fulfill a need. If I have the product that solves your problem, you will choose to alleviate your problem by buying from me.

Questions forge interaction and solid communication. Isn't that your goal as a marketer? Learn to become a Master Detective,

> ### Learn by Asking
> When you talk, you only know what you know. When you listen, you know what the other person knows, too.

Better ask ten times than go astray once.
—Yiddish proverb

Listening Finds Clues

and then teach others how to become good at asking questions, too.

IMPROVE YOUR QUESTIONING SKILLS

Master questioners are not gifted naturals. The fact is, asking questions is a *skill*, not an attribute. Attributes are characteristics that come preinstalled at birth. They can include drive, determination, positive attitude, persistence, and aggressiveness.

Skills, on the other hand, are learned. Lucky for us, we are all born with a huge appetite for curiosity. It was God's plan for us to thirst for knowledge. When we were children, we were naturally curious. That's why and how we learned as much as we did when we were kids.

Do you know how to ask good questions? You used to be a master at it when you were young! You've gotten candy, bicycles, kisses, money, back rubs, employment, and millions of other things throughout your life because of your ability to ask the right questions at the right time. And, other people have used their questioning abilities to get you to do things *their* way. He or she who asks the best questions wins!

Children question everything. They ask every form of how, why, what, when, who, and where questions. If you rekindle this old habit, you will gain the power to lead your prospect down the win/win path to

Start With Questions for Yourself

To achieve success, any person—whether a military general, a chess player, an athletic coach, or a salesperson—must ask powerful questions like:

- What have successful people in my position done in the past?

- If I were a competitor, how would I outsmart me?

- How can I best use my team's special skills against their team's unique weaknesses?

- What tools do I have in my arsenal that my competitor doesn't have?

- What would the downside be if I initiated a particular maneuver?

- How would my future change if we accomplished our mission?

- What would my spouse/family/parents think if I were successful and accomplished my mission?

Some of these questions motivate you. Some help you gain a different perspective. Some keep you focused on key points.

making a purchase, and will build your business in the process.

ASKING QUESTIONS UNLOCKS DOORS

It is your job to ask the questions that will enable you to solve a problem or fill a need that your potential client wants taken care of. Doctors and detectives ask probing questions to resolve the matters at hand. Journalists rely on questions to get their stories. You, too, must learn to again become a Master Questioner—just as you were when you were a child.

Powerful Questions Shine Light Where There Is Darkness

It's time to sharpen your questioning sword—it's time to rekindle that talent you used to apply so well. It's time you started using this tool to reach your marketing goals.

An old rule of thumb in sales is that you have one mouth and two ears and should use them in that proportion. I was taught to never use more than three to six declarative sentences in a row before injecting a question

You are going to have to become proficient at observing how others use questions in daily conversations. Have you noticed that after you buy a particular model of automobile, you start seeing lots of them on the highway? (Of course, there were lots there before you bought the car—you simply didn't pay any attention to them.) It's the same with questions. Once you become aware of the power of good

Keep a Question List

How does a person learn how and when to ask questions? (This is a good question, isn't it?)

Keep a special note pad or place in your day-planner where you keep track of all the great questions you hear. Write them down immediately or else you'll forget them. Next, it is critical that you keep these questions where you can use them during your conversations.

Eventually, you'll memorize the questions that work best as you become comfortable with them.

Questions
-What kind of information are you looking for?

questioning, you'll start to notice just how many questions people are asking one another in normal conversations.

You'll also notice that some people never use questions. They use declarative sentence, after sentence, after sentence, telling people more than they want to know and not necessarily "sharing" any substantial message.

Think back to some of the best conversations you've had. The conversations just seemed to flow, didn't they? That's the way you want your prospect to feel when your presentation is done.

We might think we got lucky and found a prospect with whom we "hit it off." Maybe we just felt that the other person was "into" the topic of conversation. If you could play back a video- or audiotape of that conversation, I'm willing to bet that at least one of you asked a lot of meaningful questions.

FORM Your Questions

Is there a difference between asking a question and asking a powerful question? Absolutely. For example, the FORM sequence (Family, Occupation, Recreation, Message—see the box to the left) was designed as a tool to remind people to initiate a "normal" conversation with a prospect before talking about their products or services.

You can use FORM-type questions to ask a prospect about their family, or about their job, or about a sports event that was on television the night before. The purpose of this line of questioning is to get a normally shy salesperson to open up to another person by initiating some level of conversation.

FORM Questions

These are topics that you can use to get people talking, build rapport, and lead into your message.

Family—everyone has one
Occupation, career
Recreation and leisure interests that you may share
Message—once rapport is established, you can talk about your sales message!

It's your mission to build rapport and then deliver a soft message about your company's products or opportunities. Here's an example of how your line of questioning might take place during the last Message stage. Embellish, as you say something like:

- "Now isn't the time to talk" [about my business]. ("Is it?" is implied).
- "You may not be interested in the fascinating business I am in. . ." ("Are you?" is implied).
- "But perhaps you know somebody who is interested . . ." ("Give me a few names" is implied!)

If you have built rapport before you deliver your message, the prospect will be curious about what you do. You started the conversation by setting them up with, "Now isn't the time to talk"—what would you say if some stranger you just met said this? You'd think, yes, now isn't a good time to talk, and might wonder if this person were a con artist. Next, we pressed on to say, "You may not be interested." Again, internally, I've gotten you to say, right again, Mr. Stranger. But if you've established just an ounce of rapport with this person, the last statement will draw them further down the road toward them hearing your presentation.

SPIN Questions

SPIN® Selling, a major sales method developed by Neil Rackham, is based not only on questions, but on asking specific types of questions in a particular sequence. SPIN starts

---

SPIN Selling

S stands for situational questions. These questions cover the basics of the buyer's situation.

P stands for problem. These questions uncover problems they may be having.

I stands for implication. These questions lead the prospect to expand the importance of the problem.

N stands for need-payoff. These questions cover the benefits of solving the problem.

with basic questions about the buyers' situations and moves to helping them see how you can help them gain many benefits.

The bigger and more important the sale, the more homework you should do about the buyers' situations, and the less patient they will be answering basic questions to educate you about their circumstances.

Studies have shown that successful salespeople spend most of their time on *Problem* and *Implications* questions. Since intelligent people understand their own problems, you succeed by acting as a consultant or trusted advisor who helps them meet their goals.

> Talk low, talk slow, and don't say too much.
>
> —John Wayne

OFFER A GOOD QUESTION, THEN LISTEN EFFECTIVELY

In order to benefit from asking good questions, you have to be a good listener. While questions allow you to make your points and demonstrate your expertise, the question's goal is often to learn about a customer or prospect. Think of listening as the establishment of a "listening post" for gathering the information you need to do business with someone.

Successful Sales

What one factor would make for successful sales? According to sales veteran John Burgess, "Listen to your customer, and everything else will fall into place."

It is extremely important for you to visualize yourself as the person in charge of manning the "listening post" opposite the person with whom you are talking. Your mission is first to gather information, then secondly to share information—*not the other way around.* How do you know what your prospects' "hot buttons" are? How do you know what will motivate them to take action? You won't know until you close your mouth and listen.

Listen More, Talk Less

Are you the "spray and pray" type of person who just brain dumps everything you know about your company, hoping you hit one of your prospect's hot buttons in the process? This is the most widely used method in marketing—and the *least* effective. This is the "throw it up against the wall and see if anything sticks" approach. Listening more effectively will dramatically improve your communications with your family, co-workers, and prospects.

Listening is not just hearing, it is:

- a method of tuning in to the communication process initiated during your business activities
- the art of applying oneself to hearing something from another person in hopes of finding a need you can fill
- placing your undivided attention on something important to your business survival
- taking notice of communication with another so as not to waste your time or theirs

Wouldn't you agree that it is hard for most people to be good listeners? On a scale from 1 to 10, how would you rate *your* listening skills? Really? Recent research shows that we take in information through four openings (our ears and eyes) and only give it out through one. So you should talk only 20% of the time.

Of course, we have a reciprocal situation here. You become a better listener by asking better

---

Active Listening Skills

Listening sounds like a passive activity, but you can actively participate in the conversation without talking at all.

- Use nonverbal signals that show you are listening: nod, smile, lean forward, and make eye contact.
- Don't think about what you are going to say next. Instead, listen for things that you can ask about.
- Give the speaker small verbal signs of interest such as "uh huh," "yes," and "oh."
- Restate the speaker's points.

questions. And *when you listen better, you can ask better questions.* It's really that simple. Set up a "virtuous cycle," rather than a vicious one where everyone talks and nobody listens. The better your questions, the more successful you will become at listening to, and understanding, the thoughts and concerns of others.

STORYTELLING

When you talk, don't lecture. When others ask you what you do, default immediately into your testimonial story. Remember, you are a *paid professional storyteller.* You should have a personal story to tell about your product or service (even if it's about a customer).

Be ready to briefly and enthusiastically share your story with new prospects. Features tell and benefits sell—so focus on all the worthwhile *benefits* of what you offer.

Stories are more effective at getting your message across than stating the message. Stories are more fun to listen to and easier to remember. People identify with them, and they make your point without generating as much resistance from the listener.

Stories Pack a Punch

Abraham Lincoln cultivated his precision storytelling into a formidable political weapon.

"If you have an audience who has the time and is inclined to listen, lengthen it out slowly as if from a jug," he advised. "If you have a poor listener, hasten it, shorten it, shoot it out of a pop gun."

During the Lincoln-Douglas debates of 1858, Stephen A. Douglas actually feared this skill possessed by his opponent. "Every one of his stories seems like a whack upon my back," said Douglas. "Nothing else, not any of his arguments or any of his replies to my questions, disturbs me. But when he begins to tell a story, I feel that I am to be overmatched."

—Donald T. Phillips,
Lincoln Stories for Leaders

QUESTIONS MOVE DECISIONS

Once you know how to obtain information from your potential clients, you will have the power and the control you need to lead your prospects into an "informed decision." With a little luck, you've made a great

31 Sample Questions

HERE IS A LARGE GROUP OF QUESTIONS TO WORK WITH THAT FIT DIFFERENT ASPECTS OF A SALES OR PRESENTATION SITUATION:

- Let me ask you a few questions and then I will answer all of yours, okay?
- Will you give me 10% of your trust and let me earn the other 90%?
- Would you get excited if . . .
- Doesn't it give you confidence to know . . .
- What is important to you about (your job, a business opportunity, your family, etc.)?
- I would like to ask you a few questions and then tell you about our company, fair enough . . .
- Who will help you make your decision?
- Why don't you take the product and see for yourself?
- Would Tuesday, Thursday, or Saturday be better for us to meet?
- Can you see the value of _____? Would that be of benefit to you?
- What kind of information are you looking for?
- Why wouldn't you just take action with me today?
- How do you know when you see a good business opportunity?
- What exactly do you mean by, I want to think it over?
- Do you mean not interested for now or forever? Please explain.
- What is your plan to get yourself there?
- What kind of money would you like to be earning three years from now?
- If the results indicated that an investment in our product only costs 85 cents per day, how could you pass up this kind of value?
- Would you be willing to go back to school for 9 months, so you could retire in 4 years with a $56,000 a year passive income?
- If ___ were no longer a problem, would you get involved?
- Would your spouse enjoy hearing about that?
- I'm inquisitive, what makes you feel this way?
- Are you committed to making a serious change? When?
- What other options are you considering?
- Are you dissatisfied with your present situation? Why?
- Do you have any questions?
- How many hours a week will you devote to building your in-home business?
- Did you see an opportunity with our company today?
- Will you be starting full-time, part-time, or just using the products ?
- What will you do to improve the second half of your day?
- Will I share this powerful strategy with everyone in my downline?

E-mail me with your great questions at DKlaybor@hotmail.com

impression on your prospects and they'll decide to take action and move forward to buy your products or services.

We want to be proactive and positive about the use of probing questions, not manipulative. We're all about helping people fill a need. Your job is to share, not convince; to share, not sell; to share, not tell. We need to use the power of questions to discover the real needs and wants of our prospects and to fulfill their wishes. In so doing, you will sell a lot.

GET STARTED ASKING QUESTIONS

There are thousands of good questions you can ask someone, but there are billions of foolish questions to ask. The box on the opposite page contains some openings and questions you can use to sell your products or services, recruit your sales force, and train others more effectively.

Use those questions and thousands of other great ones to reach all your goals, dreams, and aspirations. If you ask good questions, you could very possibly grow your business tenfold in a year.

I'm sure by now you have clearly understood the benefits of learning a few good questions to use during your business activities. I am not suggesting that you learn 100 of them, but learn at least a handful soon.

> You never persuade clients of anything. Your function is to understand the issues that matter to your clients—[and help them solve them] from their point of view.
> —An executive cited in *The SPIN Selling Field Book*

Use a Buddy System

One way to get started on new marketing behaviors is to get together with another person who shares your dream of becoming successful. Ask them to work with you using a buddy system. You both agree to hold the other accountable to learn and use a few of these questions each month. It's not hard at all. It's just a matter of having someone push, prod, and reinforce you into learning some of the questions listed.

Remember, you must continuously invest in your career. Doctors do, mechanics do—every professional does. Why would you think a marketing professional would be an exception?

Many salespeople spend more money improving the *outsides* of their heads than they do improving the *insides*! Make it a goal to attend seminars put on by the leaders of your industry no matter if they're with your company or not. Expand your mind and reap the rewards of asking better questions.

BURST INTO ACTION

To move the world, we must first move ourselves.

—Socrates

1 List the information you would like to know about every customer or prospect.

2 Develop a list of questions that will impress a prospect with your knowledge.

3 Make a list of questions, the answers to which will cause prospects to conclude that they need your help.

4 Use questions to find out what personal issues count with your clients.

5 Develop a list of how, why, what, when, who, and where questions.

6 Be prepared with questions about nonbusiness topics like Family, Occupation, and Recreation that will build rapport.

7 List Situation, Problem, Implication, and Needs Analysis questions you can use.

8 Practice your active listening skills.

9 Develop stories that make your points for you.

THE CREATION FACTOR
Beyond Customer Service

James A. Ray

James Ray is an expert in the science of success. He has devoted the last two decades to studying success factors, and gives audiences advanced strategies for accelerating results in the areas of sales, personal achievement, leadership, team performance, and life balance.

After achieving top recognition at AT&T for sales, management, and leading their national telemarketing operations, Mr. Ray moved on as a master trainer with the AT&T School of Business and to establish a four-year alliance with the Stephen Covey Leadership Institute.

He is the developer of The Science of Success,™ a series of easy-to-learn, proven methods and skills that produce outstanding, consistent results in all areas of life. Companies like IBM, Dow Chemical, RE/MAX, AT&T, Nikken, and numerous others have profited from Mr. Ray's message and methods.

Mr. Ray conducts keynote presentations, corporate training, and seminars. The secret to Mr. Ray's success is his ability to take the seemingly complex and break it into manageable, understandable, and memorable strategies for improvement.

James A. Ray, James Ray International, 7514 Girard Avenue, Suite 1-544, La Jolla, CA 92037; phone (619) 459-6909; fax (619) 459-9186; e-mail James@JamesRay.com; www.JamesRay.com

THE CREATION FACTOR
Beyond Customer Service

James A. Ray

> Success is dangerous. One begins to copy oneself, and to copy oneself is more dangerous than to copy others. It leads to sterility.
>
> —Pablo Picasso

Nothing fails like yesterday's success. Now, more than any time in our history, we must begin to adopt new approaches and new ways of doing business. Knowledge is doubling every three to five years. A good many of the things you will use on a daily basis in five years have *not even been invented yet.*

This may seem extreme, but check your own experience. Think about how many items have become commonplace in your own life that did not exist five to ten years ago. Those things that produced results in the past will no longer bring success in the present and into the future. If you are running your life or your business as you did twenty, ten, even five years ago . . . you are going out of business. (For instance, see Chapter 10.)

To be outstanding in the marketplace of the future, we must continually "re-think our thinking" in every area of our lives, every moment of every day.

THE WORLD HAS CHANGED

The world of yesterday is gone forever. No longer will customer service alone, or even excellent customer service, differentiate you in the marketplace. Again, we must re-think our thinking. Customer service and satisfaction have become the expected standard in the marketplace. To truly set ourselves apart from our competitors, we must go *beyond customer service* to the "creation factor." How do we do this?

Excellence Is Not Enough

A multitude of individuals are excellent at what they do. They are excellent at customer service and satisfying customer needs. But, 99 times out of 100, these individuals are not the people making major impact. The individuals who receive the accolades are those who are more than excellent—they are *outstanding.* Therefore, you must become outstanding in your field.

THE CREATION FACTOR

"Excellent" managers, sales people, and business owners operate very well within *current* paradigms. Conversely, outstanding leaders *create* new paradigms. In other words, they *go beyond* the current trends; they create new trends. They

don't serve and satisfy customer needs, they break through these thresholds to surprise and delight their customers by creating customer loyalty through *innovation* and *creation.*

In a world where customer service and satisfaction are much talked about, a paradox exists. We are often told things like "The customer is always right" or "We must satisfy all our customers' wants and desires." This is true, isn't it?

Maybe. I would like to submit to you that customer service is a paradox in that it is absolutely necessary, but in-and-of-itself it is insufficient. In fact, in many cases, customer service is actually a *disservice.*

How can this be?

ARE YOU REACTING, COMPETING, OR DESIGNING?

My company's mission is to ignite the entrepreneurial spirit and accelerate business growth. The objective is to assist individuals and organizations in designing and creating the lives and businesses they truly desire, both now and in the future. I will address this in a moment. But first, let's understand how the vast majority approach their lives and the outcomes they produce as a result.

> If you're not willing to impose your terms on the future, you have to be willing to let it impose its terms on you.
> —T.S. Eliot

The Reactive Approach

Many people live a substantial portion of their lives in a reactive/competitive mode. They have become absolutely excellent in this mode of operation. But unless they change their approach, they will never become outstanding.

When we live a life of reaction, we are living the *effect* of an outer stimulus. For example, a customer may want a particular service, product, or benefit. In a reactive mode, we hurriedly scramble to provide exactly what customers have requested.

We may react quickly and efficiently; we may do so with warmth and kindness. It may endear us to our customers; however, it will *never* truly set us apart or drastically increase our market share. At best, the reactive approach will satisfy and serve, but in-and-of-itself, it will *never* increase business for the long term.

The Competitive Approach

What about the competitive approach? Not only do the truly outstanding not react—they do not compete. For the outstanding creators of the future, competition *does not even exist!*

To fully understand this idea, let's look at how the competitor operates. The competitive person expends a great amount of energy and effort measuring his competition (hence the rise of the "benchmarking" movement). Competitors are constantly concerned with meeting, matching, or beating the competition.

Perceived success or failure is measured in relation to the accomplishments of others. For example, a new product or service enters the market, and those in the competitive mode rush to develop a similar product or service. Consequently, these individuals and organizations are continuously at the mercy of the few outstanding performers. They will always be searching for a way to be like, or to differentiate themselves from, the market leader—the one who *created* the new need. They are, and always will be, "behind the curve."

The Creative Approach

Conversely, when the creative, outstanding products hit the market, they become the market leaders because they "create the curve." When you create the

ORIGINALITY PUSHES
YOU OFF THE CHARTS

curve, you own the market. You stand alone in a world of reactors and competitors.

These creative few can set the market price for their products as well, since no precedent has been established. Their products are most often viewed as the top of the line or the highest in quality. Because of their foresight, they can continue to charge a premium as long as they provide and maintain a strong perceived value in the mind of the consumer. (See Chapter 1.)

Be An Original

The reactive/competitor's product is frequently viewed as a take-off on the market owner's product. And, as if this were not enough, the second and third to market typically have to compete at a lower price—versus the creative market leader who can charge whatever *they* want.

Think about it. When you consider where to go to buy athletic shoes, what comes to mind? Probably Foot Locker, the number one shoe chain in the world. Foot Locker designed and created a market; consequently, they own the market.

When you think of facial tissue, what comes to mind? Kleenex, of course. Kleenex created and now owns the market. Not only do they own the market, their brand name has become the *descriptor* of the product line.

Last but not least, when you think of buying high-end gourmet coffee—where do you go? Starbucks, of course! Starbucks is one of our country's most recent success stories—the creator, leader, and owner of their market.

I could go on and on but the point is this: Each of these creative few is doing more than satisfying and serving customer needs—they are creating *new* customer needs. As a result, they have the ability to charge a premium for their products. They create and own their markets!

SO WHAT'S THE PROBLEM?

Unfortunately, the majority of us are still caught in the customer service/customer satisfaction mind-set.

It's an okay *start* to ask our customers what they want and then provide those exact products and services. In fact, this reactive and competitive mind-set has been the major contributing factor to the entire quality movement (more on this to come).

Solving Problems Is Only a Start

Both the reactive and competitive approaches are interrelated. Often, these approaches manifest themselves as "problem solving." When problem solving, we are focusing on what *we don't want* versus designing, creating, and focusing on what *we want*.

We problem-solve all the time. But problem solving will *never* guarantee that you create or achieve what you *truly want*. And it certainly won't make you a market leader or a market owner. When solving problems, you are limited by the innovation and foresight (or lack thereof) of others—not a very empowering position from which to design your future. Let's explore this further.

Conventional wisdom, by definition, favors that which has come before. That's great if you're building a house, but it's useless—even dangerously misleading—in creative positions.
—Barry Diller, founder, Fox Television Network

WHERE'S YOUR FOCUS?

In his excellent book *Leaders, Strategies for Taking Charge*, Warren Bennis speaks of the "Wallenda Principle." You may recall the high-wire family known as "The Flying Wallendas." You may also remember that Carl Wallenda fell to his death.

An interesting interview was done with Carl's widow several months after he died. In this telling conversation, Mrs. Wallenda speaks of how her husband had always been totally fearless. She spoke of how he was always thinking of his next event, always attempting to make it bigger and better.

"It's the strangest thing though," she recounted, "something shifted in Carl." She then proceeded to tell how a few weeks before his demise, he had awakened from a nightmare in a cold sweat. "He had a dream that he had fallen to his death, and from that moment on he became totally consumed with safety." She continued, "We would see him checking the wires, making sure they were taut. He was so afraid of falling." Unfortunately, Carl's worst fear became his reality.

You Get What You Focus On

The Wallenda principle asserts that *you will move toward (and create) your continual point of focus.*

Your point of focus is critical to your outcomes. Individuals and organizations who function in the problem solving mode focus a major portion of their energy and effort upon the very things they *don't want.*

Getting back to customer service—aren't we most often fixing problems and dealing with things that our clients *don't want* instead of designing and creating what they do want or *will want* in the future? Of course we are!

This may seem confusing. However, if you will take the time to understand it, this distinction between problem solving and creating will *massively* impact upon your personal life, your professional life, and your position in the marketplace. We must understand that the results we get today are the direct outcome of the decisions and actions of *yesterday.* Consequently, when we problem-solve, we are dealing with the effects of a past cause.

People tend to move away from problems (or things they don't want) instead of defining, creating and *moving toward* what they ultimately want to achieve. Sadly, this is how the majority of individuals live their lives and make their daily decisions. Compare this mentality to driving your car while looking into the rear view mirror instead of out the windshield (don't try this, it is just a metaphor!). This type of thinking causes us to literally "back into the future with our eyes on the past."

Problem solving will never get you what you want. It will never make you outstanding in your personal or professional life. And yet, this is the typical approach to customer service. We literally do ourselves and our clients a disservice by constantly living out of memory rather than possibility.

WHAT YOU THINK ABOUT, COMES ABOUT

In 1991 I was brought into a manufacturing organization to improve employee morale, which had hit an all-time low. Although this type of request was not that unusual, when they described the situation to me, they left out one small piece of information.

It seems the entire plant was scheduled to close and the employees had been told that soon they would all be out of a job! It was obvious why morale was so low. (Talk about a challenge!)

Upon arrival, the primary point of discussion was the fact they were going out of business. At the time, I was in the early stages of making these key distinctions we are exploring, but I knew that in order to change morale, I had to help them change their thinking. They were utilizing the Wallenda Principle to their own demise.

I passionately began to tell them that they had to change their focus. I told them repeatedly, "If you continue to focus and concentrate on what you don't want (going out of business), you will tend to further it and possibly expedite it."

Believe me, this was a hard-sell. Almost every day without fail, I would encourage them to "Focus on

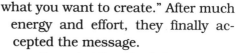

what you want to create." After much energy and effort, they finally accepted the message.

I constantly asked them, "What do you want?" When they would come back with something they didn't want, I would not accept it and would ask again, "What do you want?" We finally began to set goals. Instead of focusing on not going out of business, we began to focus on becoming profitable and getting new customers. Instead of focusing on how poorly we had been treated, we began to ask, "How can we make today a fun and productive day?"

Positive Focus Leads to Positive Results

You see, concentrating on how terrible it is that "we are closing" or the fact that "we really don't want to close our doors" was debilitating and deadly. And the fact of the matter is, they had been told they were going out of business so it couldn't get any worse. We collectively agreed to re-think our thinking by deciding that "if we were going to go out, we would go out in style." With this mentality, two things could happen:

- At the very least, they would feel good about themselves and their accomplishments.
- They may have opportunities to transfer to other parts of the business that were not closing by being highly attractive and productive employees.

Could it be possible that the situation would be reversed?

Little by little we began to see positive things occur. The primary production line met its quota for the first time in months; and this was the turning point. People began to take pride in their work again, and a new slogan started circulating around the plant: "We're going to make it happen no matter what!" Slowly we began to celebrate the small successes and talk about how to make them bigger and better. And then the big announcement came—they had recruited a new client and signed a two-year contract as a result! The plant was going to stay open.

WE'RE GOING TO MAKE IT HAPPEN NO MATTER WHAT!

It was a long road to shift the mentality of an entire organization, but I'm happy to say that they are still open and viable as a business. Part of this condition is directly correlated to the fact that they began to focus on and create what they wanted (a thriving and lasting business) versus what they didn't want.

There are obviously many factors that were involved, but the learning point is two-fold: First, we could have given good customer service by fixing morale in the short term (which could have been done in numerous ways). Instead, we used "The Creation Factor" to make a lasting difference in the organization.

Secondly, this is a great example of the Wallenda Principle. And how by changing your focus to creating what you really want, you can go beyond the mere solving of problems for yourself and your clients.

Don't Predict The Future From The Past

In a recent survey, American managers were asked, "What will it take to be successful in the new millennium?"

Eighty-five percent of the managers polled answered, "Quality."

They're wrong! Quality is no longer a highly differentiating factor in today's environment—quality, like customer service, is *expected*.

The truth is, America ran W. Edwards Deming out of our country with his quality principles, so he went where there were future-thinkers at the time—Japan. Because of this, the Americans fell behind on the innovation curve and, following the success of Japan, began playing "reactive catch-up" to the quality movement.

Ironically enough, in a management survey with Japanese managers, the same question was asked, "What will it take to be successful in the new millennium?" Not surprisingly, approximately 90% of their managers had a different answer—"new products."

Chances are that you have been exposed to or involved with the quality movement. Never before has there been a movement so widely accepted in corporate America. Guess what? Continuing to make quality a primary focus in the future is reactive—it is problem solving. This approach will not make you more outstanding!

> Many change programs are so general and standardized that they don't speak to the day-to-day realities of particular units. Buzzwords like "quality," "participation," "empowerment," and "leadership" become a substitute for a detailed understanding of the business.
> —Michael Beer, professor, Harvard Business School

QUALITY IS ONLY A START

I am by no means suggesting that quality is unimportant. Quality is imperative. But, let me ask you a question: Will quality sell your products or allow you to highly differentiate yourself from your competition? Of course not!

Likewise, will great customer service sell your products or allow you to differentiate yourself from your competition? Same answer.

Why? Because these attributes have become the norm. They are expected. Products and services must be of high quality and customers must be well served just to be considered in the market—just to *maintain* market share.

Good Service Isn't Enough

Customer service is very similar to the quality issue.

I have worked in many organizations which were heavily vested in some new customer service program. Unfortunately, they were not involved in this program because of its innovation capabilities. Rather, they were in the race to react to their customers' perceived needs or to "out-service" their competitors.

The sad truth is, when (and if) they achieve the level of customer satisfaction they are targeting, it will not provide a sustainable leading edge in the market place.

CREATE NEW ADVANTAGES

I strongly believe that if we do not begin moving toward a creative and innovative mentality, it will be the major factor that leaves us behind both in individual and business arenas. We must differentiate ourselves through creation rather than through reaction and competition. We must get beyond customer service to the creation factor.

> The best way to predict the future is to create it.
> —Peter Drucker

Those individuals and organizations who understand and apply this truth will be the leaders in the new millennium. Understanding this distinction will differentiate and catapult them into a new arena. They will have no competition in an arena and a market that *they create and own*. This is the imperative that will cause all of us to thrive versus merely survive in the years ahead.

Not Just Creativity

Many people in our workshops say, "Okay, I understand, but isn't this just about being creative?" The answer is no.

There are distinct differences between being creative and creating, even though they are

The Difference Between Creativity And Innovation

There is a distinction between "creativity" and "innovation." I don't use the terms synonymously. I think of creativity as the generative side. It's coming up with the ideas. They are a dime a dozen. There are zillions of ideas and all sorts of games one can play to elicit them from others or from yourself. That's the easy part, although for some people even that is tough. The tougher part is the innovation side. Taking the idea to the marketplace is the execution side. Real innovation is such that it not only creates a new product, it furthers the industry itself.

— Louis Patler, co-author of *If It Ain't Broke, BREAK IT!*, interviewed in *Executive Edge* newsletter

related. Many individuals are creative. They have great ideas, but they never put their creativity into *action.*

The difference is that creators have creative ideas which are followed by immediate, intelligent, and consistent action. Being a creator necessitates an end product. In other words, *creators get results!*

Creating is about bringing something out of nothing— creating a need where none is currently perceived. Creators are, and most often will continue to be, the "owners" of their markets.

An Example of Applied Creativity

General Electric holds the worldwide patent on the self-cleaning oven. This one patent alone generates literally *billions* of dollars for them. How many people would even *consider* buying an oven in this day and age that isn't self-cleaning? Slim to none. The self-cleaning oven has become a staple in our society. For those who use an oven, it is an absolute necessity.

Guess what?

No one ever asked GE for a self-cleaning oven. If GE had been reactive, they would have waited for a request—and, in all actuality, would probably still be waiting. Instead, GE was a creator—not only of a new product feature, but of a *need.* GE went beyond customer service and the competitive mindset to the creation factor.

Why Didn't They Think of That?

Let's look at an opposite situation.

Daniel Burrus, the author of the best-seller *Technotrends*, speaks of multi-speed windshield wipers. If you have purchased a new car within the last ten years, it would be a safe bet that your car has multi-speed windshield wipers as standard equipment.

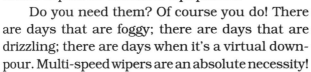

Do you need them? Of course you do! There are days that are foggy; there are days that are drizzling; there are days when it's a virtual downpour. Multi-speed wipers are an absolute necessity!

If this feature is so valuable, how is it that we had single-speed wipers for over thirty years?

Dan Burris went to the chairman of Chrysler, Ford, and General Motors and posed this very question. Guess what answer he was given?

"No one ever asked."

The point is that for over thirty years the American auto industry was extremely *reactive* in the area of wipers. Waiting for someone to ask is deadly! Think about how much potential revenue was lost with this one simple feature. All because no one asked! This is truly customer disservice!

Countless companies are asking their customers what they want. This is a faulty approach. In many cases, customers don't *know* what they want. In fact, if a customer had been asked what they wanted in windshield wipers, the answer may likely have been, "I don't know...how about blue?"

But We Could Have Thought of It!

Not only did the car companies around the world not think of the intermittent windshield wiper, but when a small inventor got a patent on it, they all stole the idea. Their defense was that it was common knowledge because it didn't involve anything new. Only after many years, did the inventor win his court case and millions in damages from every car company.

Other players skate to where the puck is . . . I skate to where the puck is going.
—Wayne Gretzky, hockey great

TAKE THE INITIATIVE

Market leaders are creators. They don't ask the market what they want, they create new needs. They *tell* the market what they want!

That's why they are leaders. When you are measuring and following the market, you are invariably following one or more of the market leaders.

I'm not suggesting that measuring customer satisfaction and needs should not be done, only that it should not be viewed as sufficient. *Satisfying* customer needs is reacting. *Generating* customer needs is creating.

Becoming a creator is about becoming a futurist. It's about looking ahead and creating a need where none is currently perceived.

HOW TO BECOME A CREATOR

How do we make this shift? How do we design and create customer needs? How do we get beyond customer service to the creation factor?

Creating this begins with a shift in our habitual thinking. This is where our leadership and consulting practice spends a large portion of its time. Although there is no way to teach all the methodologies in this one chapter, there are three things you can begin to put into practice immediately.

Questions for the Innovation Generation

1. How can I best provide for or satisfy this need?

2. What is the cause of this need? Or what purpose is this need satisfying?

3. How can I provide more value by addressing the cause of this need?

4. What is a different or a better way I could do that?

5. What is another example of that? (Continue asking yourself until you run out of ideas.)

Your Current Approach

First, you must understand your normal tendencies and your normal approach. It is important to honestly assess your current way of operating before you can begin to consider a different way.

One thing is certain: We are all doing everything absolutely perfectly to get the results we are currently getting! To get different results, we must re-think our thinking—and more importantly, follow new thought with new action!

The Pareto Principle (80/20 Rule)

The majority of us spend approximately 80% of our time problem solving. This will *never* set us apart.

Remember the 80/20 rule? The rule basically says that 80% of our results come from 20% of our efforts. If we apply the 80/20 rule to our day-to-day activities, we will find that we are typically problem-solving 80% of the time and spending no more than 20% of our time innovating and creating.

Even though problem solving is where most of our energies and efforts are spent, we make the assumption that we can surprise and delight our customers with this approach. This is faulty logic.

Remember the Wallenda Principle—you move toward your primary point of focus. Put another way, "What you think about, comes about."

Don't Be Reactive

Second, realizing that reaction and competition is the norm, you must begin to break your old patterns of thought behavior. You will then be able to develop new habits which will foster your creative ability. This is not as easy as it may sound. I consistently spend a great deal of time with

> The definition of insanity is doing the same thing over and over and expecting a new result.
> —Albert Einstein

What! No Problem Solving?

Many people ask, "Are you suggesting that problem solving is something we should *never* do?" Not at all. But just suppose for a moment you were to flip the percentage.

What would happen if you spent 80% of your time innovating and creating and 20% problem-solving? How much would that improve your business and your results? How would that improve your personal life? Obviously it would make a *dramatic* difference! As we begin to spend 80% of our time innovating and creating, and no more than 20% of our time problem-solving, we will be guaranteed that the Wallenda Principle is working in our favor. This is truly the *creation factor.*

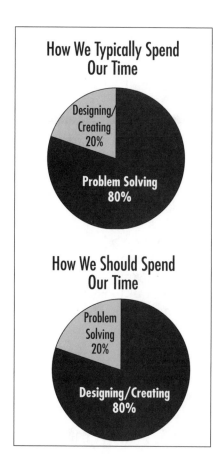

How We Typically Spend Our Time

Designing/Creating 20%

Problem Solving 80%

How We Should Spend Our Time

Problem Solving 20%

Designing/Creating 80%

this very issue when teaching our Science of Success seminars to individuals and organizations.

Designing and creating what we want is not how the majority think. I challenge you to become a student of yourself and others, and I guarantee you will find this to be true.

Ask the Right Questions

When I ask someone what they want in their organization, a frequent response is, "Well, I *don't want* all this fighting and lack of teamwork." I will respond "Wait a minute, that's not what I asked you—what do you *want*?" Or I may ask, "What do you want in your job?" Often the answer is something like, "Well, I know I *don't want* to work for this boss any more!" Once again I will respond, "That's not what I asked you—what do you *want*?"

Create Positive Images

The Million Dollar Question?

What do I really want?

Unfortunately, this is not only present in question and answer scenarios. Audit your language and the language of others. How frequently do we tell our children, "Don't spill the milk."

Now think about it: What do they have to focus on to make sense out of your request? They have to access a visual image of what you don't want them to do! What if you said, "Make sure to keep all the milk in the glass."

Or how often do you tell a guest when leaving your home in the dead of winter, "Don't slip on the ice"?

What visual image do they access? Instead, what if you said, "Walk carefully on the ice." These positive outcome statements may sound a bit strange at first, but think about the images they create versus those of the first statements. Is it possible these positive statements would create a much greater success ratio?

I wonder how often, because of our way of thinking and communicating, we set the Wallenda Principle in motion to the disadvantage of ourselves, our loved ones, and our clients. You can never truly become an outstanding creator—you will never skate to where the puck is going—until you first break out of this ineffective pattern.

> Problems we face today cannot be solved with the same level of thinking we were at when we created them.
>
> —Albert Einstein

Change Your Thinking

The first step in this process is listening to your own language and auditing your own thinking. When you catch yourself focusing on what you or your customer *don't want* versus what you *do want* (and you will), you must interrupt the old pattern and begin to condition a new habit.

I challenge you for the next thirty days to commit to heightening your awareness of your language and your thinking. As you begin to notice your old disempowering patterns, immediately re-think and re-state what you *want* instead of what you don't want.

FOCUS ON FUTURE POSSIBILITIES

Finally, we must follow the immortal knowledge of Albert Einstein and realize that "Imagination is more important than knowledge."

Put another way, we must begin to live out of imagination rather than memory. No longer can we afford to limit ourselves by what we have achieved or created in the past. I like to say, "We must not re-live the past but pre-live the future."

Imagination is more important than knowledge

The past *does not* equal the future.

We must become the Wayne Gretsky's of our industries. Like General Electric, we must begin to anticipate customer needs; but even more importantly, we must create new customer needs. To do this we must overcome our own self-imposed limitations. We must discontinue our reactive/competitive problem-solving behaviors and begin to utilize our true capabilities.

CONCLUSION

It is widely known that we only use 10% of our true potential. You must begin to tap into your human uniqueness and power by believing in yourself and trusting your intuition.

If you understand and apply this, you will join the ranks of the absolutely outstanding in the new world ahead. You will begin to create, live, and work in a world where there is no competition. You, and you alone, will lead and *own* your industry.

The rare individuals and organizations that operate this way will set the standards. They will create the curve, and they will have the abundant rewards that follow. Be one of them!

BURST INTO ACTION

First comes thought, then organization of that thought into ideas and plans; then the transformation of those plans into reality. The beginning, however, is in your imagination.

—Napolean Hill

1   List things that you are doing that you know are habits from the past. Commit to dropping the ones that are unproductive.

2   Great customer service is a good basis for success with your current approach. What could you do that would immediately improve things for customers? How about speed up responses, offer a great guarantee, call your best customers now, or provide more value?

3   Analyze any segments of your business that are shrinking. Is there anything you can do about them? Are they profitable to ride down?

4   Analyze the segments of your business that are growing. Do they represent new trends that you can ride up?

5   If you could create the ideal new product or service, what would it be? How can you move toward it now?

6   Create a customer advisory group. Ask them what an ideal new product would be for them. Talk to customers who have complained or left. Do their reasons give you any new ideas?

7   Hold a brainstorming session with a cross-section of your employees (include customers, suppliers and others if you're too small). Explicitly ask for the wildest ideas, craziest ideas, and ideas that could never work. Often these will be your jumping-off point for a breakthrough product or service.

8   Instead of competing with competitors, how can you partner with them? Call three today and set up a lunch with at least one.

9   What are you focusing on now that you're trying to avoid? Change your negative focus to a positive focus regarding something you want to accomplish.

10   If you started a new business today, without any investment in your old infrastructure, what would it be? Why not start creating that new business now?

Chapter 7

MILLION-DOLLAR NETWORKING

Sam Wieder

Sam Wieder, MBA, is a consultant and trainer who helps business people develop their potential for personal success. He helps his clients dissolve public speaking anxiety, speak with greater impact, and break through their barriers to greater success and income. His Million-Dollar Networking workshops show business owners and sales organizations how to cultivate win-win, business-building relationships.

An accomplished trainer and speaker, Mr. Wieder is a Certified NLP Trainer and has been recognized by Toastmasters International as a Distinguished Toastmaster. He has presented workshops in the United States, Canada, and Europe. He is also the creator of the audio tape program Wake Up and Win.

For over 17 years, Mr. Wieder has addressed a variety of business and professional audiences. He has been a keynote speaker for the International New Product Exposition and the International Association For Financial Planning. He has also presented programs for Westinghouse Electric Corporation, Consolidated Natural Gas Company, the International Personnel Management Association, and the American Society For Training and Development.

Sam Wieder, M.B.A., 860 Harrison City Road, #5A, Greensburg, PA 15601; phone (724)832-7459; fax (724) 836-8606; e-mail Samsalive@aol.com.

MILLION-DOLLAR NETWORKING

Sam Wieder

Giving people a little more than they expect is a good way to get back a lot more than you'd expect.

—Robert Half

When I entered the world of professional speaking, I thought I could be a one-man marketing machine. Was I ever wrong! Unfortunately, I found this out the hard way.

My struggles began when I first tried to promote my public seminars. I mailed out flyers. I placed ads. I posted announcements on public bulletin boards. And what did all of this get me? Not much. In fact, I lost money time after time. No matter how much I marketed, I couldn't attract more than seven people. I wanted to cry.

What went wrong? I didn't really figure this out until I asked myself a different question: What went right? What had I done right to attract the few people who did attend my seminars? The answer had to do with the magic of personal relationships. Most all of my seminar attendees were either people I knew or people referred by people I knew. They came as a result of networking!

THE POWER OF NETWORKING

Sparked by this "Aha!", I began a quest to discover how I could harness the power of networking to attract enough seminar registrants to pack a meeting room. I read every networking book I could find. I joined a networking group. And with the help of that group, I launched a grand experiment to test the marketing power of networking.

My idea was to conduct a networking seminar as a fundraising event. With the group and I teaming up as 50–50 partners, we would promote the program almost entirely through networking. And that's just what we did. There were no costly advertisements, no expensive mailings to cold lists. I simply trained my fellow group members to promote our seminar to their circle of contacts and then turned them loose.

Magical Results

What were the results of this experiment? By the night of the seminar, we had a total of 64 registrants, only about a quarter of whom were members of the networking group. What's more, only one attendee came from the dozen or so free announcements we had placed in area newspapers. The rest were from networking.

Was I excited? You'd better believe it. Before this, my best-attended public seminar had attracted only seven registrants. But by harnessing the power of networking, I had boosted that total to 64—over nine times as many!

How would you like to multiply the number of new clients or customers you are attracting by

> The key to making networking a marketing team effort lies in joining networks.
> —Paul and Sarah Edwards,
> *Teaming Up*

nine times? Or even three times? Through networking, you can.

Plant Some Seeds

Before you can harvest a rich crop of customers through networking, you must first plant some seeds. What kind of seeds? This is something I discovered by chance a few years back when attending a course to be certified as a stress management instructor.

Everyone in that class but me was either a chiropractor or some other type of holistic health practitioner. Feeling at a disadvantage among so many health experts, I tried to compensate by making an extra effort to contribute to the class in the best way I knew how—as a speaking coach. I praised all the strong points of my classmates' presentations. I readily shared speaking and training techniques to help everyone improve. I became excited about helping my classmates be their best. Soon even the instructor was turning to me for feedback and advice. I was a cheerleader, mentor, and coach all rolled into one—and I had a ball.

Months later, I got an unexpected phone call from the head of the organization that had certified me as a stress management instructor. He wanted me to teach their first European seminar. Wow! How did this happen? This wasn't the kind of opportunity that had ever just dropped into my lap. There were about a hundred other instructors who were certified to teach this course— yet, he had called me. Why?

I'm convinced that the deciding factor was what happened in my instructors' class months earlier. I had stepped beyond the role of being "just another student" and freely shared all that I could to help make my class as successful as it could be. Sure, I had the demonstrated skills to do the job I was being asked to do. But what set me apart from the others is that I gave so freely of myself to support the success of my class. Although I didn't realize it at the time, my efforts to help others were seeds I was planting, seeds that would eventually sprout and bring me a rich harvest.

Embrace a Spirit of Unconditional Giving

As I thought about this experience, I began to wonder. If embracing an attitude of giving for that one week led to my landing an exciting European training assignment, what might be possible if I lived my whole life with a spirit of unconditional giving? How many golden relationships might I establish? How many other exciting opportunities might I attract? And how satisfying and exciting would it be to see how much I could help others become more successful?

In marveling at these possibilities, I had tapped into the essence of effective networking—helping others succeed. That is one of the fastest ways to cultivate productive relationships. And it's easy to see why. When you help others, you show that you care about them. This not only commands their attention better than the slickest marketing brochure but makes you the kind of person that others are eager to help in return.

In short, the more you give, the more you get. If you want to make millions, start by giving away millions. You don't have millions to give away? Think again. Whatever your financial net worth, I'm willing to bet that you command at least one million dollars worth of resources. And the sooner you make a habit of effectively sharing these resources with others, the faster the riches will come flowing back to you.

> High-performance networkers gain endorsements for reasons that go beyond the basic product or service. They do extra—ordinary things.
> —Thomas J. Stanley, *Networking with the Affluent and Their Advisors*

MILLION-DOLLAR RESOURCES

What million-dollar resources do you command? To find out, play different roles. Take your pick. Mix and match. Here are the roles you can play to scatter your seeds of success and catapult yourself to the status of a million-dollar networker.

ROLE #1: Prospector

When I was just getting started as a speaking coach, each new client was like a rare golden nugget. So when a friend put me in touch with an executive who needed some help in fine-tuning a business presentation, I was thrilled. Would I have even been aware of this prospective client if it weren't for my friend? Probably not. But because my friend was out there prospecting for me, he was able to send me a new client.

You can do the same for your business contacts. Everyone you meet is a prospective customer for someone. And one of the greatest challenges in business is attracting new customers. How easy would it be for you to find new customers for business people you want to help? Just think of yourself as a prospector who is constantly looking for customers for others. A new customer is quite a gift!

The Million-Dollar Question

An excellent question to ask people you meet at a networking function is, "Who would be a good customer for you?" This question sets you apart from everyone else who asks "What do you do?" and gives you the information you need to help them.

ROLE #2: Purchasing Agent

Your business contacts are often looking to buy quality equipment and supplies at a reasonable price. By acting as their purchasing agent, you can help. Just ask yourself what businesses you know that could do a top-notch job of filling their needs.

Let's say you've just purchased a computer. Before making that purchase, you looked through eight different catalogs and visited four area computer stores. Through your exhaustive research, you were able to find a dynamite price on the most cutting-edge business computer system. How useful would your research be to someone else who needed a system similar to yours? How much time and money could you save this person by sharing what you learned about where to find the best products and prices? By acting as a purchasing agent for your key business contacts, you can help them in a way that they'll truly appreciate.

ROLE #3: Talent Scout

One of the greatest challenges of many businesses is finding and keeping good employees. Screening and hiring the right people can be costly and time-consuming. How much do you think your business contacts would appreciate it if you could help them lessen this headache? By thinking of yourself as a talent scout, you can help them. Just keep your eyes open for talented people who may be a good match for the needs of your networking contacts.

8 am	Prospector
9 am	Purchasing Agent
10 am	Talent Scout
11 am	Matchmaker
12 pm	Intelligence Officer
1 pm	Mentor
2 pm	Sounding Board
3 pm	Cheerleader
4 pm	Endorser
5 pm	Publicist

I was talking to the manager of a staffing firm that was trying to fill several customer service positions for a major bank. Thinking of myself as a talent scout, I then passed along the staffing firm's information to a contact who was actively seeking the type of position being offered. A few months later, I was gratified to learn that my contact had indeed landed a job with the bank.

By acting as talent scout, I had helped two people at once. Through my referral, the staffing manager filled a position and my friend had a new job. Both greatly valued my help—and it only took a few minutes of my time. What businesses do you know that are seeking skilled help? Step into the shoes of a talent scout. The talent all around you is a big part of your bank of million-dollar resources.

ROLE #4: Matchmaker

A few weeks before I was to give a business networking seminar in my area, I went to a Chamber of Commerce mixer. On the welcoming committee was Gwen, a member of my networking group. I knew relatively few people at this event, but with Gwen's help, that soon changed.

After introducing me to someone she knew, Gwen said "Sam is giving this great networking seminar next month. He'll be happy to tell you more about it." Gwen would then disappear, having primed the conversation and given me the opportunity to talk about my seminar. A few minutes later, she returned to introduce me to someone else. Gwen was superbly playing the role of matchmaker, paving the way for me to meet many more of the people I wanted to meet than I would have otherwise.

Million-Dollar Matchmaking

Introduce:
- your clients to their prospects
- your suppliers to your colleagues
- business newcomers to veterans

Which individuals do you know who could benefit from meeting one another? Get two of them together over lunch. Or introduce them to one another at a networking event. You could even bring your networking contact as a guest to your business or professional association meeting and introduce him or her to many potentially useful contacts. By acting as a matchmaker, you can help create million-dollar connections for others.

ROLE #5: Intelligence Officer

Business people need information to survive and prosper in today's competitive marketplace. Simply by being who you are, knowing what you know, and traveling in the circles that you do, you possess or have access to much more of this information than you may realize. By sharing this "intelligence" with your networking contacts, you offer something of great value.

> **Share Your Intelligence**
> • articles, books, tapes
> • upcoming seminars
> • useful Web sites
> • marketing opportunities

The intelligence you share can take many forms. You may find an article describing a market trend that directly affects a contact's business. Maybe you know of a commercial building for sale that would make a great new store location for an expanding company. Perhaps you discovered something that your contact's major business competitor is doing that would be useful for him to know. Or maybe you know of a book or seminar that would be of great interest and benefit to many of your contacts. Act as an intelligence officer and share this information. When you do, you'll be giving away something that others will appreciate.

ROLE #6: Mentor

My first full-time job was selling insurance on commission. Getting started in this field was, for me, no easy task. With little sales experience of any kind, I was as green as they come. So I really appreciated it when a more experienced agent named Buzz took an interest in me and served as my mentor. Whether I had a technical question or sales challenge, Buzz was only too happy to share his knowledge, experience, and advice.

I'll always remember that. Many years after I left the insurance business, that memory motivated me to track down Buzz when I needed a health insurance policy and to refer others to him as well.

You surely have business or life experience that has led you to where you are today. You've made mistakes. You've struggled at times. You've learned things along the way. How useful would your knowledge and experience be to others who are just starting to do things you've already done? How many mistakes could you help them avoid? How much time and effort could you save them? Be a mentor and share your advice. Others will appreciate your support.

ROLE #7: Sounding Board

When I was developing my first educational audiotape program, I needed feedback on my script. Was it clear and understandable? Would it hold people's interest? Did it work? To get answers to these questions, I read a portion of my script to my Toastmasters club—a group I can always count on for constructive feedback about my speeches and presentation skills.

Judging by the confused or blank expressions on my club members' faces, I quickly knew that much of my script had missed the mark. Based on comments and suggestions from the members, I revised the script. Shortly thereafter, I read the revised script to the group, and was delighted at how well it worked. By using my Toastmasters club as a sounding board, I gained invaluable feedback. This not only saved me the expense and embarrassment of releasing a dud into the marketplace, but helped me produce an audio program that people would want to listen to again and again.

You too can provide invaluable help to your business contacts by acting as a sounding board for their ideas. Volunteer to listen to their business ideas and share your opinions. Offer to evaluate their marketing materials. Without feedback from

> Up the proverbial creek? If you've got a network, you've always got a paddle.
> —Harvey Mackay,
> *Dig Your Well Before You're Thirsty*

others, it is often difficult to see the flaws in our own ideas or approaches. By acting as a sounding board for others, you'll help them see things more clearly, make better decisions, and more quickly succeed in reaching their goals.

ROLE #8: Cheerleader

The last time someone sent you a note of congratulations or complimented you on something you did well, how did that make you feel? Being recognized and appreciated feels great. Yet there aren't nearly enough people out there leading the cheers for any of us. You can be different. By being a cheerleader for those in your circle of contacts, you will lift their spirits and give them something that is priceless.

What can you find to cheer about? Plenty. When one of your contacts wins an award, mail out a quick note of congratulations. Do the same when someone you know has given a great speech, published an article, written a book, started a new business, gotten married, or given birth to a child. Maybe you'll see someone you know mentioned or featured in newspaper article. Clip it out and mail it to the person with a short note that says something as simple as "Well done!" or "You're famous!"

Perhaps you admire someone's persistence, dedication, thoughtfulness, or sense of humor. Or maybe you are impressed with how skillfully someone has solved a problem or handled a challenge. Praise all that you admire in others. The better you are at recognizing the accomplishments, special occasions, and talents of others, the easier it will become for you to play the role of cheerleader.

> We wildly underestimate the power of the tiniest personal touch. And of all personal touches, I find the short, handwritten "nice job" note to have the highest impact.
>
> —Tom Peters

ROLE #9: Endorser

Shortly after I produced my first professional audiotape program, I was struggling to get some written testimonial comments for my promotional materials. The program itself was well received. It was just that most of my early customers were either too busy to listen to the tape right away or too busy to write out their comments after they did.

One exception was Rick. He sent me two full pages of positive, specific, enthusiastic comments that effectively highlighted the major benefits of listening to my program. And that wasn't all. He was so excited about my tape program that he loaned it to two of his friends—and they gave me great testimonial quotes as well. This was a marketer's dream!

I truly appreciated the time Rick took to do that for me. So much so that I have sent him job leads, helped him with projects, and shared my advice and encouragement to support his success. Yes, I was only too willing to return Rick's favor and more. His endorsement meant that much to me.

Who has provided you with a product or level of service that you could readily endorse? Who do you know, in particular, who is just building a business and could truly benefit from your endorsement? Sing the praises of that person or business in a testimonial letter. Highlight the specific benefits you received. Be as positive and enthusiastic as possible. Do this and—believe me—you will be remembered! To someone just building a business, a good testimonial letter is marketing gold.

ROLE #10: Publicist

I once sent a friend a promotional flyer for one of my upcoming public seminars. A week later, he called me and said, "I'm sorry I can't make it to your seminar. But I did fax a copy of your flyer to 20 of my contacts who I thought might be interested. I hope this helps boost your attendance."

How do you think this made me feel? I was elated. Promoting a public seminar was a real challenge on my own. But here was someone who took the time to publicize my event—and I hadn't even asked him! He had, in effect, served as my publicist.

What events are your contacts trying to publicize? How could you help promote someone's business among your circle of contacts? What publicity opportunities can you help create for others you want to help? Think of yourself as a publicist for others, and you will win their appreciation and enter the big leagues of million-dollar networking.

A REAL-LIFE MILLION-DOLLAR NETWORKER

One shining example of a million-dollar networker is Art Gifford, an accountant interviewed by Dr. Thomas Stanley for his book *Networking With the Affluent.* Always on the lookout for ways to help others, Mr. Gifford often negotiates the purchase of homes and automobiles for his contacts, sells products and services on behalf of his clients, and helps his contacts locate suitable credit sources. As both a resource and advocate for others, he also maintains a list of quality suppliers, shares advice on business-related problems, and promotes and endorses his contacts and their causes.

And what has all of this seed-planting done for him? In just 11 years, Mr. Gifford built a company that started with only three CPAs into a firm that has over 800 clients and employs 34 CPAs, along with a support staff of almost 20 other types of employees. He's never had to make cold calls, and has had 34 affluent new clients referred to him in a single month. Mr. Gifford truly knows what an abundant harvest is possible when you make a habit of planting seeds by helping others.

THREE KEYS TO ATTRACT SUCCESS

By helping others succeed, you'll set into motion a wave of empowerment. And just like an ocean wave that rolls out from the shore, an incoming tide is sure to return. But how can you be sure that this returning tide brings you what you want? How can you attract what you most need to help your business grow and prosper? To do so, you must take three key steps.

> Relationships determine success.
> —Philip B. Crosby, *Quality is Free*

1 POSITION YOUR BUSINESS FOR SUCCESS. Helping others succeed will inspire them to help you in return. But even if they want to help you, they can't effectively do so unless they know how. As you might imagine, this knowledge isn't going to just magically pop into their heads. You have to put it there. To do so, you need to clearly, memorably and consistently communicate your business identity to the world.

Begin by creating a positioning statement—a single sentence that tells what you do, who you do it for, and how you do it differently or better than others. Focus on the problems you solve or the benefits you provide. Incorporate this positioning statement into a 15–30 second mini-commercial you can give whenever anyone asks you what you do. Build upon this by sharing your business success stories whenever you can. Your objective is to lock your business identity into people's minds.

I help others achieve _____ by _____.

The more clearly and consistently you communicate your business identity to the world, the more easily you will attract an abundance of customers, referrals, and the support necessary to ensure your success. (See also Chapter 1.)

This law of attraction works even greater wonders when you're busy helping others. And it's easy to see how. As a million-dollar networker, you'll send many cards, letters, faxes, and e-mail messages, all of which will say "Here's some help!" When you help others, they'll feel good about you. And when your messages of help also contain a consistent visual reminder of what you do (be it a company logo or business card), they'll link that good feeling with your business. This will not only ignite their desire to help you but will remind them of how they can best do that.

Help Others Understand and Remember Your Business

- If you're in business for yourself, select a business name that effectively conveys what you do.
- Design your company logo, business card, stationery, and marketing materials to reinforce your desired image.
- Feature your logo and possibly your company slogan on your fax cover page and in your e-mail signature.

2 **TARGET THE PEOPLE YOU WANT TO INCLUDE IN YOUR NETWORK.** To gain the most benefit from all you are doing to help others succeed, concentrate on helping those who are best able to return the kind of help that you most need. Provide your help with absolutely no expectation of getting anything immediately in return. You're not helping in order to "get something." That will quickly turn others off. You're helping in order to create the possibility of establishing a relationship in which help and support can flow freely both ways. That's the mindset you must embrace.

In a spirit of giving, seek to establish as many mutually beneficial relationships as you can. Trust that some of them will blossom. If you and your networking contact each have an abundance of resources that are truly useful to one another, you can create networking magic. You have the basis for an ongoing relationship that fuels your mutual success.

I recently established a great networking relationship with Jane, the owner of a new meeting and event-planning company. I was excited to meet Jane because we had so much to offer one another. I got her involved in my networking group to help her expand her circle of contacts. I gave her the contact information for the local chapter of Meeting Professionals International so she could network with other meeting planners. I took her to my National Speakers Association chapter meeting to meet speakers she might be able to hire in the future.

Jane, in turn, started sharing what she had learned about networking over the Internet, something I'd been thinking about adding to my networking seminars. She also suggested the possibility of using me as a seminar speaker. We had a lot to offer one another—and this is what made our relationship a million-dollar connection.

You too can make million-dollar connections by focusing on establishing relationships that have the greatest potential to be mutually beneficial. Who are your ideal customers? Who has great access to your ideal customers or others who would be useful for you to know? Where do these people gather or what organizations do they belong to? When you know who you want to meet, go where you are most likely to find that type of person. This will greatly increase your chances of making million-dollar connections.

The Odds Are Up for This "Bookie"

One accountant combines his love of reading with networking.

The accountant segmented his referral sources into A, B, and C. The dozen As are lawyers and bankers who refer to him regularly. He knows their interests well. One way he keeps in touch is by sending them books on topics that fit their individual interests. He puts a sticker in the books saying they are thank-yous from him.

Two or three times a year, he sends the same book to his complete list of 50+ contacts. (He buys at a discount from the publisher.) Referral business is up almost 20% in six months.

—Rick Crandall
1001 Ways to Market Your Services: Even If You Hate to Sell

3 COMMIT YOURSELF TO EXCELLENCE IN WHAT YOU DO. When you commit yourself to business or professional excellence, you make it easy for others to support, publicize, endorse, and refer customers to you. So do whatever you can to strive for continual improvement. Keep learning. Strive to understand and meet the changing needs of your customers. Commit yourself to serving your customers well. This commitment will multiply the abundance that comes back to you as a million-dollar networker.

BURST INTO ACTION

An ounce of application is worth a ton of abstraction.

—Booker T. Washington

1 Make a list of the types of business people or professionals you would most like to be a part of your million-dollar network.

2 Make a list of your current contacts whose professions are included on the above list.

3 For each of the above contacts, identify the million-dollar networking role you could play that would best help that person at this time.

4 Define exactly how you will play each of the above roles.

5 Play each role as you have defined it to start giving away your millions.

6 Send me a postcard when you've made your first million.

SECRETS OF SUCCESSFUL REFERRAL SOURCE MANAGEMENT

Jim Rhode

Jim Rhode, BME, CSP, chairman of SmartPractice, has developed and presented hundreds of seminars and workshops on practice administration and professional marketing for three decades. He has spoken to thousands of progressive professionals, and their spouses and staff members.

From his years in industry as a long-range planner with American Can Company and Celanese Corporation, Mr. Rhode brings to the medical profession scores of practice-building techniques and the motivation for timely implementation. His extensive business experience includes team building, financial analysis, operation streamlining, and long-range planning.

He is a member of the Society for Advancement of Management, and the National Speakers Association. Mr. Rhode was honored with the prestigious Arizona Entrepreneur of the Year award for 1990. He has given talks in all 50 states, and 13 foreign countries. In addition, he is the publisher of *PracticeSmart: Dentistry's Marketing and Management Newsletter*.

Jim's philosophy is best summarized by the proverb: "Any enterprise is built by wise planning . . . becomes strong through common sense . . . and profits wonderfully by keeping abreast of the facts."

Jim Rhode, SmartPractice, 3400 East McDowell, Phoenix, AZ 85008-7899; phone (602) 225-9090; fax (602) 522-UFAX.

Chapter 8

SECRETS OF SUCCESSFUL REFERRAL SOURCE MANAGEMENT

Jim Rhode

> Satisfied customers are an organization's most successful salespeople, because they do not stand to benefit financially from recommending the organization to others.
>
> —Eberhard E. Scheuing,
> *Creating Customers for Life*

G etting referrals is the most effective marketing you can do. Most companies wish they had more referrals, but they don't have a program to produce them consistently. Generating new referrals can grow your business in the new millennium. This chapter will show you how.

WHAT YOU WILL LEARN IN THIS CHAPTER

In this chapter, you will learn proven secrets of successful referral source management that will work in your business.

- seven reasons why clients refer
- seven reasons why they don't

- eight actions you must take to keep customers wanting to return
- nine ways to make your office or business more "client-friendly"
- five dramatic concepts to differentiate your business from others
- eight ways to encourage your clients, staff, and friends to refer

At the end of this chapter, you will also find 10 Action Secrets you can put to work in your practice or business today to increase your bottom line through effective referral source management.

HOW *WHAT* YOU LEARN WILL INCREASE YOUR REFERRALS

Using the strategies presented here, you will be able to significantly increase your business through referrals by:

- implementing cost-effective ideas immediately;
- reducing or eliminating those concepts that don't work for you;
- using word-of-mouth marketing to your best advantage.

WHAT IS WORD-OF-MOUTH MARKETING?

Word-of-mouth marketing is creating an experience that will keep other people talking about you. For example, a friend of yours comes into your office and happens to mention what a fabulous meal he had last night at a new restaurant in town. His positive influence or recommendation—his word-of-mouth endorsement about the restaurant—might significantly influence you to try out that restaurant in the near future.

Word-of-mouth marketing tools can keep others talking about you, too. For example, if you provide a novel value-added giveaway, such as an imprinted gift, it will give the recipient something to mention to his or her friends in normal, everyday conversation.

SEVEN REASONS WHY CLIENTS REFER

First, it's important to know why your existing clients refer others to you. There's no real magic to it, just common sense. Here are the seven reasons I have found why clients give referrals.

1 **They are the referral type.** In other words, they are sociable, like to be liked, and enjoy helping other people. Often, these are the most successful people in business.

2 **They expect referrals in return.** If they own or run a successful practice or business, they look to other professionals like you to help increase their business. One hand washes the other!

3 **They like you (somehow, you really pleased them).** People like others who treat them well, often by pleasing them with excellent service or by delivering a greater than expected result. Some of your best referrals sources are the people you pleased the most— people you've really helped in a crisis or time of need.

4 **They like a particular part of your business.** The likelihood of repeat business and referrals often lies in how your staff treats customers. I cannot underscore this principle enough! In a landmark publication (*Marketing Strategies: A Guide to Practice Growth*), Stephen W. Brown, PhD, renowned professor at Arizona State University, presented the concept that:

A Legend In Their Own Time

Nordstrom department stores encourage employees to satisfy customer needs that you wouldn't expect. Their goal is to create word-of-mouth legends—about their services.

Just how legendary Nordstrom's service has become was shown by the results of a survey in Phoenix. Residents were asked to name their favorite department stores. As usual, Nordstrom was number one. The extraordinary thing is that Nordstrom didn't have a department store in Phoenix!

- 68% of lost clients are the direct result of staff discourtesy
- 16% are lost due to product/service dissatisfaction
- 11% are lost to competitive inroads
- 4% simply move away
- 1% pass away (see diagram)

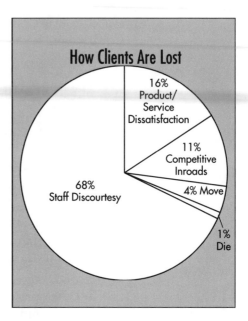

How Clients Are Lost

16%
Product/
Service
Dissatisfaction

11%
Competitive
Inroads

68%
Staff Discourtesy

4% Move

1%
Die

Imagine if every business in America reduced that 68% to 0%!

5 **They think you are fair and competent.** Most everybody I know likes to feel treated fairly, in both business and personal relationships. They also enjoy a sense of security being in the hands of a competent practitioner or professional.

As one neighbor of ours recently commented, "When I sit in Kelly's chair (she happened to be referring to her stylist), I know that I will be well taken care of. She's an excellent hair dresser. I wouldn't leave Kelly for anything!" She'd follow Kelly to a new shop. This is the classic, word-of-mouth type of referral.

As long as Kelly's fees remain fair in the market and she continues to deliver the same high level of competent service, my neighbor will never leave her salon! And, what's more important, she'll make lots of referrals to Kelly!

6 **You are convenient and easily accessible.** People on the go today like things quick and easy. That's why more fast-food restaurants prepare complete family meals that can be picked up on the way home after a long day at work. That's

why grocery stores are going back to offering home delivery. That's why franchises are springing up on every busy intersection. Customers who find it easy to get to you, with ample parking and no hassles, are more likely to (a) keep coming back and (b) refer their friends.

7 **You refer to them first.** The notion of reciprocity is not a new one. Setting up a mutual referral system is a quick, easy and painless way to generate more referrals. It's fair and it works!

SEVEN REASONS WHY THEY DON'T REFER

You'd be surprised to discover why people don't refer to you!

1 **They think you are already too busy.** Tell them the truth— that you always welcome new customers. People move, retire, etc.

2 **They think you are too expensive.** Tell them you're in the "high-average" fee range. Truth be told, although people say they look to low price first, psychologically, they're afraid of it for fear that quality will be compromised.

3 **It never occurred to them to refer.** Plant the seeds in their minds that you welcome referrals from people as nice as they are.

4 **They think you are "elitist" and don't care to do business with "rank and file" society members.** Discuss this with them.

5 **They don't refer to anybody—ever!** They are afraid to be responsible for a mismatch that would reflect poorly on their judgment. Now's a great time to suggest it—when they feel most satisfied with your service or product line.

6 **They don't want to share you with others.** They like and want to keep your exclusivity. You need to reassure them that they'll always be a "preferred client."

7 **They're afraid that if you get too busy, you'll lower your quality or level of service.** That's why they want to keep you for themselves! Actually, that's quite flattering, isn't it? But, if you need new clients, this reason can hurt you, so identify and discuss this "business-buster."

EIGHT ACTIONS YOU MUST TAKE TO KEEP CUSTOMERS WANTING TO RETURN

Now that you know why your best clients refer to you and why some don't, you need to know what you must do to keep them wanting to return.

1 **Believe in your quality and service level.** As one of the basic criteria for the Malcolm Baldrige Awards, commitment to continued quality and improvement is essential for all businesses and services to grow and to continue to thrive in the future. If you don't commit to quality, why should anyone refer you?

2 **Be convinced that your customers or clients need what you present to them.** Who is better and more qualified than YOU to know what your customers need and want, and what is in their best interests over the long-term? One of our best customers recently shared with me that when he gives a case presentation, he always includes a preface that goes something like: "If you were my mother/wife/sister/daughter/father/brother/son...I would recommend _____ because that's what is best for her/him." His case presentation acceptance rate is well above 80%! Note: This works only if you mean it.

3 **Focus on the benefits to the client as a result of "buying" what you have to offer.** This will vary, of course, depending upon the type of business or service you run. Some of the most successful marketing messages include: quality, endurance, self-indulgence ("you deserve the best"), increased satisfaction with self or performance, enhanced desirability, and feelings of power or control.

Benefit Messages
- Quality
- Endurance
- Indulge yourself

Dealing With Terrorist Customers

One of the rules at Disney is: If you argue with a customer, you're fired! But as we all know, there are people out there who will test anyone's patience. If one comes into your store or office, you and your employees should be aware of a technique called "fogging." Instead of getting upset or challenging the person, you can cool the person's intensity by saying things like: "Yes, that might be true" or "That's really interesting." This keeps you above the fray. It's like pouring water on the person instead of adding fuel to the customer's fire.

After such an encounter, employees should also be able to "take themselves out of the game." They need to know they can take time to re-energize.

—Ken Blanchard

"You'll be able to strut your smile," a highly successful cosmetic dentist tells her patients with confidence.

4 All of your personnel must be courteous, even when difficult situations present themselves. Face it, we've all had to deal with difficult people—paying customers—we'd just as soon went elsewhere. They make our day miserable. We can't seem to please them to their level of satisfaction. Staff, especially, often feel caught in the middle because they must strive to be pleasant and facilitating, often acting as a "gate-keeper go-between" of the business owner and the customer. Reaching a satisfactory level of performance expectation is both a skill and an art!

One of the most successful things I've found is to turn their concerns into a question. "So do I understand that you're upset?" By acknowledging their concerns, they will feel listened to, that you care, and they will relax.

5 Ask questions to establish rapport. I make it a point to ask open-ended questions, showing an interest in the other person. This gives me time to make assessments, to learn what's really important to the other party, and to make some mental notes of ways I can present solutions that can help him or her. (See also Chapter 5.)

6 Avoid showing anger or frustration. This isn't always easy. When I feel myself getting tense or angry, I attempt to empathize with the other person. I hold my breath and count slowly from one to 10.

I try to look at things from the other person's point of view by reflecting what he's telling me. I recap the situation by saying something like this, "John, help me understand this. I hear you telling me that you're upset about _____. Is that correct? I'm sorry this happened. Let's work together on this to reach an amicable solution. Will you work with me on this?" It almost always works.

> ### Fire Customers
> If you can't satisfy a difficult customer, fire them! This will empower your staff who have been hassled by this customer. Plus, it will clear room for the quality customers you deserve.

7 **Give them your full attention.** How many times have you been "served" by uncaring people? If you're like me, the answer is "All too often." It's irritating and frustrating to have to wait your turn, only to have a service representative treat you like a non-person.

As one client's long-time office manager remarked to me at an entrepreneur's dinner one evening, "When a patient is in my doctor's dental chair, that patient is the most important person in the world at that time. My doctor strives to make each and every patient feel that way. That's why my boss is so successful in getting and keeping patients."

Wow! What a wonderful feeling, to be treated as if you are the most important person in the world! We all like to feel that way!

8 **Say "thank you" often!** One of the greatest feelings in the world is feeling appreciated. Think how often it made a difference to you when someone expressed appreciation for your effort or input.

A podiatrist client of ours recently shared a story with me about his success. He recalled having worked as an operating room technician early in his career. He had assisted a podiatrist in a particularly long and grueling operation. At the conclusion of the operation, the surgeon looked him directly in the eye and said, "Thank you, Jack. This operation would not have been a success without your help."

"To this day," said the podiatrist, "I think of him often and how his skill and his sense of appreciation helped me become a successful doctor today. There's not a day that goes by that I don't thank my staff or my patients. They make my success possible."

NINE WAYS TO MAKE YOUR OFFICE OR BUSINESS MORE "CLIENT-FRIENDLY"

Another element of successful referral management is making your business more "client-friendly." Everybody likes doing business with friendly people, from fast-food restaurants to dry cleaners. Your business is no exception. Here's how:

1 Make sure all of your staff members wear name tags. The expense is minimal and the return is immeasurable! Customers and clients feel more comfortable when they know who they are doing business with. Instead of "the tall fellow behind the service counter" or "the redhead who does my nails," putting a name with a face makes people more accountable and more approachable. It's a friendly sort of feeling.

2 Hang pictures of your staff on the wall of your business. This makes you more human to clients and prospective clients. It increases your "hospitality factor." It's nice to know what people who will be serving you look like.

A newsletter subscriber of ours has named his photo display, "Dr. Kramer's Hall of Famers." Car dealers and supermarket chains are especially good at providing employees' pictures. But just about any business can do this.

Staff photos are on display in the emergency waiting room at a Kaiser Permanente hospital. In this situation where patients will likely be treated by a doctor they haven't dealt with before, it's easy to imagine that patients might be put more at ease even while they're waiting, seeing the faces of the staff who will be treating them.

3 Make sure your reception area is wide open and airy. Gone are the days of fogged, sliding glass doors with a mysterious employee lurking somewhere in the shadows. Today's service industries are warm, friendly, open, approachable. They set goals, for example, to acknowledge everyone who enters within 30 seconds!

4 Provide a comfort level of background music. It helps people feel at ease. Psychologically, it puts them in a relaxed state of mind by mentally transferring them somewhere else. If you're unsure about the type of music best suited to your clients' tastes, find out by asking them. You can include a question or two on your client survey, or simply ask them at a service point.

Gauging your audience and adjusting to their preferences can have a dramatic effect on your business and in generating new referrals.

A Client "Music Questionnaire"

1. Did you notice the music in our office?
   - ☐ Yes
   - ☐ No

2. Was the volume...
   - ☐ too loud
   - ☐ too soft
   - ☐ just right?

3. Please rank order your preference from the following:
   - ___ classical
   - ___ contemporary
   - ___ country
   - ___ disco
   - ___ gospel
   - ___ show tunes
   - ___ opera
   - ___ New Age

An office manager in Colorado called me recently, frantic as to what to do. It seemed her boss preferred very loud rock music, to the point of distraction for the staff and patients. She asked me what I could recommend.

I suggested they discuss developing a patient satisfaction survey at their next staff meeting. They came up with a variety of questions about the levels of service provided in their office. Mixing in one question about the music and weighing the results from the fact-driven perspective of paying clients could make a dramatic impact upon the doctor's preference for loud rock music.

The office manager called me back two months later. It seemed that more than one-third of the patients mentioned the loud music. The doctor, somewhat reluctantly at first, agreed to turn it down for awhile.

5 **Create a "living" environment in your reception room or intake area.** We all like to feel comfortable in the living rooms of our own homes. It's true in many professional settings, as well, and can generate increased referrals.

Many professional practices feature fish tanks (proven to reduce blood pressure); or scenic videos of wildlife, nature scenes, crackling fires, rain forests, or ocean sound effects. Living environments serve as focal points of interest that gently distract customers from some of their anxieties or inhibitions.

The focal point of a professional group practice in Tempe, Arizona, features a built-in aviary with several dozen colorful breeds of feathered friends. Clients, and especially their children, enjoy watching and listening to the birds, which are housed in a safety-glass-enclosed, climate-controlled, professionally cared for environment.

6 **Have a professional logo that carries throughout every aspect of communication with your clients.** For example, scrubs or uniforms, your stationery and business cards, your billing invoices, your newsletter, shipping labels, your doormat and your outdoor signage. You will be surprised at how much people do notice!

A successful client of ours in Spring, Texas, told me recently, "My patients comment positively every day about my staff's matching, professional look. Carrying a logo throughout the office has been a great boost to my practice," said the doctor.

7 **Provide cosmetics and "creature comforts" in your reception area and rest rooms.** Customers will be impressed with your forethought and consideration for their comfort. Such amenities as scents to hide medicinal smells, a boot tray and umbrella stand in cold climates, designer hand soaps, hair spray, alcohol-free mouthwash and complementary single-use toothbrushes in the rest rooms all send a message of "We care about your personal comfort."

A prosthodontist friend in Santa Fe, New Mexico, gives patients warm, lemon-scented towels to refresh their faces at the end of impression appointments. "This is one thing I wouldn't dare give up," he says, "patients like the lemon towels so much, they'd say something if I didn't offer them anymore."

8 **Have a "no waiting" policy in your "reception" room.**
Whether in a restaurant or scheduling a haircut, we all like to be acknowledged and taken care of promptly. A pediatric dentist in Sierra Vista, Arizona, has the perfect system worked out. Even if he has several children already seated in the treatment rooms, he always has his assistant admit children promptly at the appointed time. He provides an assortment of video games,

"It's our waiter. He's stuck on the George Washington Bridge— would we care to order drinks while we wait."

tapes, and other hands-on activities for the children while he finishes up his current patients.

The parents and grandparents in the reception area like it because their children are taken in on time. The kids like it because they have lots of fun things to look forward to in the treatment area. And the doctor likes it because he doesn't feel rushed when running behind schedule. "It's a 'win-win' situation for everyone!" he says.

9 **Call "serious" or "involved" clients throughout a job or service.** Many doctors call their patients at home the evening of an invasive procedure just to see that they're doing all right. A neighbor of ours who runs one of the most successful floor covering business in the Phoenix area makes a personal site visit to every installation, regardless of the size (from the Biltmore Hotel to a guest house) just to make sure customers are being taken care of courteously and that his workers are doing a satisfactory job.

Most restaurants also make it a policy to have their servers inquire within 90 seconds to three minutes of placing an order in front of the patron if the meal is satisfactory and is there anything the patron requires. Simple, isn't it? And you can bet they get repeat and referral business through word-of-mouth marketing from satisfied customers!

FIVE DRAMATIC CONCEPTS TO DIFFERENTIATE YOUR BUSINESS FROM OTHERS

Distinguishing your business from others will also keep referrals coming your way.

1 **Understand the "out of sight, out of mind" syndrome.** To keep clients referring to you, you have to stay in front of them *between* professional contacts.

DEAN JAMES, DDS
Taking Care
of Your Smile

One of the easiest ways to do this is with cost-effective, personalized giveaways they'll associate with you. Items such as a personalized mug filled with flowers or jelly beans delivered to their workplace or car sun shades (great because they're seen by everyone in the mall parking lot every time they're used) are all great ways to keep your name in front of people. Personalized calendars, key rings, and magnets "stick around" all year, too!

2 Keep your workplace updated. Keep your "operation" in style. The look of your workplace is a direct reflection on your business savvy and currency within your profession. If your business look seems outdated, clients may perceive your business practices as equally outdated!

If in doubt, ask several of your closest friends or business associates to do an informal "walk-through" of your establishment. Ask them to play devil's advocate by pointing out things a first-time visitor might notice. Be sure to thank them, especially, for pointing out ways you can improve your business's look.

3 Be generous in all things. Be willing to go the extra mile. I like the term, "lagniappe"—meaning a small gift given a customer by a merchant at the time of a purchase. It is an unexpected extra. In marketing and merchandising, the term is "value added." I also like to call it a "Cracker Jack"—something you get free when you get down to the bottom of the box.

Think of that "new car smell" at the car wash that's added at no extra charge; or a baker's dozen at your favorite bagel shop; or chocolates on your pillow at a fine hotel. Today's professionals are learning from yesterday's merchandisers! Face it, everyone likes a free gift or an unexpected courtesy.

4 Feed word-of-mouth marketing. Be willing to ask for favors from others in the form of referrals, just as you are willing to give referrals.

5 Recruit and keep a well-trained staff. In most professions, the staff members are the first and last contact for clients. They can "make or break" your business in a hurry!

One Person Sets The Tone
by Tom Peters

Our staff is loaded to the gills with résumés to die for. Then there's Leslie McKee, the receptionist. I've never seen her résumé. But she has taken our company and turned it around. You see, Leslie is amazingly upbeat, courteous, funny, patient, upstanding and professional, smart, outrageous, and helpful. I don't know what our official "core values" are. We've never written them down. (Whoops.) But I know what they are unofficially: They're Leslie.

CUSTOMER SERVICE WONDER

Clients love Leslie. She, of course, is our Commander-in-Chief of Client Service. Among other things, she takes most incoming calls. Here's her customer-service magic:

Her manner per se—energetically cheerful—gives us a foot in the door with whoever is calling. Leslie makes sure you end up talking to the right person (no small thing), or are otherwise handled efficiently and effectively and feel good about it.

Once a week or more, it seems, she takes some totally amazing personal initiative to research something for a client. Often as not, it's unrelated to anything we do; it's just plain helpfulness. (Reading "praise Leslie letters" from clients eats up a lot of my time these days.)

© 1995 TPG Communications. Reprinted with permission of Tribune Media Services, Inc.

Hiring the best, being fair, and rewarding equitably ensures low turnover of valued and loyal staff. Make a long-term investment in them by offering to sponsor their continuing education, upgrading their existing skills, and by expressing your appreciation to them. As an employer, it is to your benefit to share your vision and to empower them to support it.

EIGHT WAYS TO ENCOURAGE CLIENTS, STAFF, AND FRIENDS TO REFER

By now, you've discovered that much of the success of referral source management lies in common sense. Here are ways to encourage referrals from clients, staff, and friends:

1 **Ask them!** Develop your own technique, with which you feel most comfortable.

2 **Reward them each time.** Remember that behavior that gets rewarded gets repeated.

3 **Thank them.** A simple verbal thank-you may be sufficient. Other times, a written note or card from you may be just the right touch. Try to send an unusual card that will be saved or displayed and has your name, logo, address and phone number in full view.

4 Extend a "$0" fee or "no charge" at their next visit; or at least consider it, depending upon the type of business you're in.

5 Refer business to them. Everyone likes to feel he or she is getting what he or she wants or needs. Help them get it. To paraphrase Zig Ziglar, "Eventually you'll get what you want, if you help enough other people get what they want."

6 Give them your magnet or picture frame to hold pictures of their children, pets, or grandchildren as a thank-you for referring. They'll look at it forever! (Remember, out of sight, out of mind.)

7 Reward them with something special for a certain number of referrals. For example, employees can receive dinner for two, flowers, theater tickets, etc.

A client of ours has generated more than 600 new patients from referrals during the last 12 months. To acknowledge and thank them, he sends a personalized letter of thanks and informs the referral that he is making a donation in that person's name to a local charity. Wow!

8 Be sure your staff know that client referrers are "VIPs" of your business, so staff will give them proper recognition and attention. Acknowledging staff referrers also reinforces the message.

Other Referral Sources

COMPETITOR REFERRALS

Some of your best referrals can come from your apparent "competitors." For instance, general practice dentists will refer to orthodontists. One landscaper gets more than half his business from a tree and a patio contractor.

"TIPS" GROUPS

In most communities, groups exist just to provide members will referrals. These organizations are often called "Tips" or "Leads" groups. Only one person per business category is allowed to join to avoid competition. Members are required to bring a lead for someone to each weekly meeting.

The Most Aggressive Referral Program

You should have at least one friend or client who will open his or her Rolodex to you and send a letter to everyone who could use your services. (You can do the same for them.)

—Rick Crandall, *Marketing Your Services: For People Who Hate to Sell*

SAMPLE LETTERS PROVEN TO ENCOURAGE, REINFORCE, AND THANK REFERRALS

Through the years, I've also found that referrals need to be tracked and reinforced. It's crucial that you keep a computerized list of your top 10 referral sources, monitor it periodically, and always, always, always, take time to express your thanks.

Following are excerpts from one of our best-selling books, *The Complete Dental Letter Handbook: Your Fingertip Resource for Practice Communications.* You are welcome to adapt and add to them to suit your professional needs. We've received rave reviews on them and I'm confident you will, too.

Dear Betty,

You recently referred (name of new client) to our office. Referrals like this are the nicest compliments we could receive. We appreciate your confidence in us.

Through referrals by patients like you we have created a positive work environment. A thank-you seems hardly enough for your trust and consideration.

Thank you for your confidence. It's our pleasure to give you the best available care.

Sincerely,

John Dentist

Dear Judy and George,

You are two of our most valuable patients! We again have the opportunity to thank you for referring (name of new client) to our office. You express so much confidence in our practice by these referrals that we would like to extend a special thanks to you.

We would be honored to treat you to a complimentary dinner for two at (name of restaurant) at (location). Just present this letter to the manager and have a wonderful dinner--on us!

My staff and I hope you enjoy this evening out. Thank you again for your continued confidence.

Sincerely,

Susan Doctor

BURST INTO ACTION

There are risks and costs to action. But they are far less than the long-range risks of comfortable inaction.

—John F. Kennedy

Following are Action Goals you can put to work today to begin your successful referral source management program. You'll have success using common sense, staff commitment, and a solid philosophy of word of mouth marketing.

1 Get your staff involved—hold a brainstorming session to generate ways to generate referrals.

2 Schedule a staff meeting to review how you provide high quality and good service—use examples from happy customers or satisfied patients. Collect written testimonials to use.

3 Reward staff—encourage and reward all ideas, not just the ones you actually implement.

4 Set target dates with new business goals—by _____(date) we will experience a (percent) increase in new referrals. We will track the source of all new client referrals and reward them promptly.

5 Implement a referral source tracking guide (see sample on page 246)—to track and reinforce referrals.

6 Have a surprise contest—give a prize to the staffperson who comes closest to naming the top 10 referrers to your business.

7 Make a list of professionals you feel comfortable referring to— create a list with phone numbers.

8 Identify one of your top referrers—invite him or her to have lunch with your staff as a special birthday present.

9 Make a list of 10 people who your practice or business needs to thank—then do it for special reasons.

10 Order a quantity of appropriate giveaways—this will keep your name in front of your client base.

Bonus Tip: Use the guide on the next page to track referrals and your responses.

REFERRAL SOURCE TRACKING GUIDE

"Whom may we thank for referring you to our office?"

When tracking your new patient sources use the following letters to denote referral codes:

P – Patient
D – Other Dentist
DS – Dental Specialist
ST – Staff

M – MD Referral
W – Walk-in
YP – Yellow Pages
O – Other

Use the following letters to denote the thank you action taken:

1 – No Action
2 – Thank-You Note/ Card
3 – Flowers to Workplace
4 – Flowers to Home

5 – Poster
6 – Restaurant Gift Certificate
7 – Professional Courtesy
8 – Other

DATE	NEW PATIENT'S NAME	REFERRAL CODE	REFERRAL NAME	THANK-YOU CODE

TRADE SHOW MARKETING

Donna Reeve

Donna Reeve
is president of The Proscenium
Group, a show management
production and consulting company. She attributes her success to helping clients
manage knowledge, strengthen efficiency of day-to-day operations and synchro-
nize strategy, technology, process, and people.

Some of her past clients include General Motors, Adobe Software, IBM,
Sunset Magazine Special Events (Time Warner), and ZD/Comdex.

Ms. Reeve is a graduate of the University of California with a BA in Liberal
Arts. She built a career in marketing and event planning, and worked several
years at an executive level as a vice president of operations in the wholesale gift
show industry. In 1989, she was awarded the designation of Certified Exposition
Manager (CEM) from the National Association of Exposition Managers.

Shortly after founding her own company, she produced and managed the
"first ever" environmental product/informational trade/consumer show in the
United States in San Francisco. The event was noted for its visionary approach
following the 20th anniversary of Earth Day.

Donna Reeve, The Proscenium Group, 1325 3rd Street, San Rafael, CA 94901;
phone (415) 456-3622; fax (415) 456-3509; e-mail: DonnaReeve@
compuserve.com

TRADE SHOW MARKETING

Donna Reeve

For the year 2000, estimates are that the economic impact of trade shows will be about $100 billion.
—Center for Exhibition Industry Research

L iz Lauter was struggling to build her business. She had sold her line of hand-painted fabric tablecloths to one of the finest stores in San Francisco. The store displayed her tablecloths in their window for a month. She even received publicity from a major newspaper article written about her designs. The store reordered once, but then sales tapered off and she was back to square one. She had spent lots of time and energy, all for one customer and a one-time event targeting the audience of that store.

Liz needed a new marketing approach to grow her business. Her budget was limited and, if she were to survive, she must find the most productive way to gain new customers. I advised Liz Lauter Designs to exhibit in industry-specific trade shows where she could maximize her efforts.

Trade show exhibitions are more effective in achieving sales and marketing objectives than business-to-business advertising, direct mail, and telemarketing. The cost of closing a sale from a trade show is 45% less than closing a sale from a direct sales call. Fifty percent of orders placed after a trade show require no follow-up phone call.

Liz Lauter took my advice and found a series of marketplaces that were ideal for her products: wholesale gift shows. Within five years, Liz Lauter Designs was writing $1.2 million in sales a year.

Trade Shows Work

Liz's success story is not unusual. For example, in Chapter 11, Ford Saeks recounts how he was about ready to give up on his product when he exhibited at a trade show and orders started rolling in.

Attendees Are Qualified Prospects

Trade show attendees have already qualified themselves as buyers: They've invested time and money to attend the show. The numbers back this up:
80% of attendees are decision makers or influencers.

90% of the attendees have not been seen by your sales force within the last year.

90% plan on making a purchase within the next 12 months.

—Center for Exhibition Industry Research

Nine out of 10 attendees rate exhibitions as the most useful source for purchasing information because they can examine and evaluate competing products in one location. More than 75% of attendees find new suppliers and ask for price quotes, and 26% purchase products. But trade show success is not guaranteed—unless you approach this marketing method with a plan to maximize your impact on potential customers.

At the annual Las Vegas Comdex show, which is the world's largest computer show, it is not

Play in Another League?

Consider displaying not only at trade shows in your field, but also at those which are in any way connected with what you do. For example, an architect who likes to design kitchens might take a booth at a gourmet food trade show, or a lawyer who specializes in employment problems might set up a small display at a personnel executives' conference.

—Michael Phillips and Salli Rasberry,
Marketing Without Advertising

unusual for some exhibiting companies to spend in excess of $2 million for a five-day event. We are talking about some serious preplanning and follow-up to justify that kind of marketing plan! Of course, you can get great, cost-effective results at most shows at a fraction of that cost. This chapter will show you how.

More than the Show

When most people think of trade show marketing, they think of exhibiting at a show. However, your success at a trade show comes largely from work you do *before* and *after* the show.

When you decide to exhibit in a marketplace, your key to success is clearly dividing the tasks at hand into three simple categories:

- before the show
- during the show
- after the show

WHAT TO DO BEFORE THE SHOW

Research the Show and Identify the Audience

Trade shows, consumer shows, and special events have become big business in the past decade. Every show promoter is competing to start new events. As a potential exhibitor, research show management and their audience. Find out information about their events such as how many years in business, how many of this particular show has this company produced, what are promotion plans and budget, past attendance figures, and demographics of attendees from the past show. If possible, attend a show to observe. Find a show directory and contact some of the listed exhibitors. Ask them about their experiences and, most telling, whether they plan to exhibit again.

A few years back, a company produced a Government Supply Show. Supposedly, the head of this company had a previous government job in purchasing. His brochure promoted the idea that he had the contacts to bring large purchasing agents to his event. He claimed this event had already taken place in several other cities and was very successful.

He lied! The reality was that as he sold exhibit booth space, he paid off previous bad debts for other unsuccessful events. There was no budget to promote the current show. Exhibitors came to display on the show dates and the show promoter was nowhere to be found. Few attendees showed up. The exhibitors banded together to sue this promoter, but he left town.

If the hapless exhibitors had spent an hour calling exhibitors from past shows and researching the company's claims, they would not have attended the show. Of course, this is an extreme example. But it's not unusual for promoters to spend more time and money selling booth space to exhibitors than they do to attract attendees.

> **Exhibitor Due Diligence Checklist**
>
> ✔ past history
> ✔ past exhibitor references
> ✔ repeat exhibitors
> ✔ sponsorship
> ✔ attendee lists

Plan Your Budget

For first-time exhibitors, budgets are difficult because there are so many new and unknown types of expenses. Many show management companies offer budget checklists that will help you assess all your costs. With proper budget planning you will avoid running out of money for key items necessary to complete your successful participation, and you will avoid a large debt at the end of your event.

Save by Sharing

If you're unsure about exhibiting at a particular show, either because it's a new show or you're not sure you can sell enough to pay for a booth, you can often share a booth with another exhibitor. Some shows offer a half-booth rate and assign you to a booth with a partner. Many shows, however, don't do this, and you'll have to call other exhibitors to try to find a partner.

Another option is to make arrangements with an exhibitor to display and sell your products for a percentage of sales.

Sudden expenses can cloud your overall experience. When I was consulting with exhibitors during the Sunset Home Show, many small companies were overwhelmed with the union rules in the exhibit halls. One exhibitor showed up intending to install his own display. He had hired his own crew of workers for the day. The local display union members would not allow nonunion workers in the building. The exhibitor was forced to hire union help at straight time rates for move-in and overtime rates for move-out. The final dollar amount was literally several thousand dollars and a budget miscalculation that ruined his show projections.

Get a Good Location

In many cases, the best shows have specific exhibit areas where they place new exhibitors. Be proactive in your efforts to directly communicate with show management about obtaining the best space available. Register as early as you can.

Learn about the exhibit hall to understand the flow of traffic. If you can, visit the exhibit hall when a show is going on. Study the traffic patterns. When visitors enter, do they tend to start with the aisle directly in front of them, or do they start at an outer row? The aisle in front of the entrance may be busiest, but if crowds are large, the mass of people might keep visitors from approaching your booth, and the noise level will be higher.

Check the exhibit hall map for locations of support posts, ramps, and other architectural features. You don't want to be surprised to find a pillar right in front of your booth that the attendees have to walk around.

If there is more than one exhibit hall, your position in a particular hall is less important than the hall itself. For example, the San Francisco Gift Show has expanded their exhibition to a third exhibit hall that is located 15 minutes from the two main areas. Many buyers save time by focusing their attention on exhibits in the two halls that house the more established vendors. Traffic is almost always noticeably less in ancillary locations. Be aggressive about asking about cancellation lists for switching to a better location at the last minute. Remember, as in retail, it's location, location, location!

Location Considerations

- Usually corner locations are preferred because there is cross traffic. More attendees notice your booth.
- If every attendee is a potential customer, locate near the entrance or concession areas. If your target market is more select, avoid these areas where attendees tend to mill around, thus making it harder for others to see your display.

Develop a Master Plan

Once you have contracted for exhibit space in a trade show, you should create a calendar timeline of tasks to complete before the event. If you are working with a team, this is the time to have a meeting and review goals, production tasks, and administrative tasks. Arrangements—everything from travel and hotel reservations to printing handouts—are usually done better and more cost effectively if they're not done at the last minute.

Show managements will provide an *Exhibitor Manual* that gives you guidelines to preparing for the event. Read this document early on and make sure you understand the materials. There are usually forms that are time sensitive and they need to be scheduled on your calendar.

There will be time limitations to your move-in for a show. This information will be in your *Exhibi-*

Early Planning Cuts Costs

Read your exhibitor packet carefully. It will contain information about reserving tables, chairs, backdrops, wastebaskets, and other props, as well as orders for utilities and set-up, and break-down labor. There is almost always a discount for ordering in advance, so it pays to plan ahead.

At large exhibit halls, you'll likely be required to use union-only labor. However, if you have a small exhibit, you may be able to set it up yourself. These regulations will also be spelled out in your packet. They're often along the lines of, if you can hand carry your materials in and set up within a half hour, you can set up your display yourself.

tor Manual. Your display design should take this into consideration. You will have to orchestrate move-in and set-up. Freight, electricity, decorating, telecommunications, lots of boxes, and staffing all have to come together.

Plan Your Booth Display

A good display will set you apart from other exhibitors and attract buyers' attention.

Many exhibitors have poor signs. People only take one second to see what your booth has to offer. Make sure your sign says exactly what benefits you offer to attendees—in most cases this is more important than the company name. Imagine that you are walking down the aisle at a busy trade show and you see a big sign that says Ackwood Corp. If you know what Ackwood Corp. does, you might decide to glance at their booth. If you've never heard of Ackwood, chances are you'll walk right on by. If their big sign said, "The Easiest-to-Use Personal Planner with the Most Features," they would attract a lot more people.

Companies can spend anywhere from $2500 to $600,000 for prefabricated booth units. However, with some creativity, there are simple, low-cost ways to create an impressive image that will bring orders.

For instance, I consulted with a company that needed a display for the Furniture Market. They had a budget of $300. Their product line was framed sculptures from Taiwan. In the exhibit hall, they contracted a wall location at the end of an aisle. They purchased three inexpensive hollow doors from a building supply and hinged them together. With a Z-shape bend, they became a free-standing wall. The doors were then wallpapered with an Oriental-reed paper that created a background atmosphere.

The sculptures were placed on freestanding columns in front of the screen. Spot lighting on each sculpture gave a museum quality to the display. It was very simple, but very effective, and the items sold out during the show. Retail store windows often have minimalistic displays that offer great ideas.

Set a Theme

Use a creative design theme and carry it forward in all your design efforts for the show. With the amount of advertising distractions in our society today, attendees respond well to continuous imagery that stimulates their memory. There is a concept known as "look and feel." Similar graphics will be designed for direct mail pieces, stickers, promotional handouts and follow-up literature. Within those graphics, certain art elements and colors will be used to create booth props.

"Exhibit memorability" has established itself as a valuable measurement of gauging exhibit success. Besides your displays, other factors that add to memorability include size of exhibit, product demonstrations, celebrity visits, and stage or theater presentations.

In the early 1990s, a show became famous for their leader-

So Easy a Child Can Use It

A photo-retouching software manufacturer hired a young-looking 15-year-old to demonstrate their software at a trade show. The youngster drew a lot of attention and made the point that the software is intended for home use.

ship in this concept. Interop used their designs to create props and graphics that created a total environment for the attendees.

Props were laser cut out of foam and stood 15 feet tall. Outside banners wrapped around the surface of the convention hall. Signage encircled columns, and the entrance to the event was an experiential tunnel of lights and marketing messages. It made the show an experience

Last year I attended a show where Lucent Technology built a 1200-square-foot stage for theater performances from the Tony-award-winning musical "Rent." At the annual Sports Show in Atlanta, exhibitors fly in cheerleading teams from all the NFL football teams and have hundreds of professional athletes there to represent their products.

> **Hot Tips for Exhibitors**
>
> *Cold Facts, Hot Tips* is a video for companies who want to achieve greater results from their exhibit activities. It is produced by show managements, exhibitors, service companies and exhibit hall facilities. To buy a copy of this video, contact: CEIR at (312) 808-2347 (e-mail:ceir@aol.com).

Plan Booth Conveniences for Staff

Show hours are long and opportunities for breaks are slim. If you expect top results out of your staff, you'll want to give them some break time that is not under the eyes of the public.

If you will have lots of staff, you might want to reserve a separate meeting room for breaks (it can double as a private meeting room to close deals with your big customers). Another option is to build a small private area within the display area.

Decide on Advance Promotions

There are several preshow marketing opportunities to catch the interest of attendees. The most common preshow opportunities for marketing include:

- advertising in trade magazines
- direct mail
- publicity in show promotor's newsletters and other mailings
- press releases

Direct mail before an event can easily double the effectiveness of your exhibit. Often a list of preregistered attendees is available. Also mail to your own customers and prospects. You can invite your best contacts to private parties and other events. But everyone can be reminded to drop by your booth. One way to encourage this is to send a coupon good for a special gift—or send half of a nice premium item so visitors must come to your booth to pick up the other half.

Some trade show events also sell marketing and promotional opportunities (MPOs). At shows like Comdex or the Gourmet Show, exhibitors are sold the rights to put their logos and messages on banners and a myriad of sponsorships that take place during the event. Some of these extras may be good for you *if* you can garner a lot of attention with them, but many are not cost-effective.

Plan Handouts and Advertising Specialities Carefully

Most handouts end up in the garbage! If you want your handouts to be kept, make them useful. These might be "10 Tips for Savings" on a wallet card, or advertising specialties that people really want. Create promotional materials or items that will remind the attendees about your products.

Giveaway Considerations

Know what you want your giveaway to accomplish. If your goal is to build name recognition, you might want to offer low-cost items like balloons or candy to all visitors. If you want to reward qualified prospects for taking the time to stop, choose a more valuable item. Remember:

- Useful gifts are more likely to be retained.
- Items that sit *on* a desk are better than items that are kept *in* a desk.

Many times a small item with logo branding is the most effective use of your budget. Years ago, Oracle participated in a show with an advertising campaign using the idea that their customers should keep "an eye on the market." At their booth, they had a big barrel of golf ball sized eyeballs with the corporate logo. Pretty soon, every attendee was walking around with those eyeball handouts. It was the show item to get.

Arrange for Booth Staffing

Staffing is directly related to the size of your exhibit space. You need enough people to handle the booth during the peak periods of the show; however, do not overstaff and create a cramped atmosphere. Attendees will feel trapped if they are surrounded by too many people representing your company.

Many times, "volunteers" are coerced to go to a show. Find people who are good at working a crowd. Let them model good performance. Try rewarding booth staff for best lead, best customer question, best testimonial, most leads, and so forth. Make it fun.

Make It Easy for Reporters

Reporters are busy and have short attention spans. Put what you do or your "hook" on the *outside* of your press kit so they can understand your message at a glance.

—*Executive Edge* newsletter

Build Your Press Kit

Effective press kits include some or all of the following documents:

- tailored cover letter
- press release (your news story)
- biographies
- collateral samples
- interesting photos
- relevant article reprints
- disk or CD-ROM containing above materials

IT'S SHOW TIME

You've invested a lot of time and money to prepare for the show. It's time to produce results.

Be Ready for the Unexpected

As with any show business production, plan for the unexpected. One of my clients had finally gotten an appointment—after more than a year of trying—with a major department store buyer. They arranged to meet at my client's booth at the show.

My client had learned to always arrive early to set up and inventory the display merchandise. This was particularly important this time because one box was missing—the box that contained the product line needed for the meeting!

My client had time to have a duplicate set of samples sent overnight to the show. The buyer viewed the products and placed the first order for $40,000. Imagine the potential lost sale if my client hadn't been organized!

> It is better to be prepared for an opportunity and not have one than to have an opportunity and not be prepared.
> —Whitney Young, Jr.

Train Booth Personnel

The most important factor is your sales staff. Come prepared with a list of goals, rules, etiquette, and general information.

If at all possible, meet with your staff the day before the show opening. However, if time and budget do not allow that meeting, make special arrangements with show management to arrive early at the exhibit hall.

Training should occur in the booth. Your staff can review and ask questions. Proper training and attitude for your staff is crucial. Be specific about where they should stand, how they should dress, no eating rules, and so forth.

The most valuable thing you can do is to train your staff to greet visitors as they are walking by. Train them in comfortable ways to engage visitors and passersby and you'll double your success rate.

Over the years of visiting show events, I am always amazed that you can walk through a show and see sales staff sitting in the rear of a booth reading the morning newspaper or eating. Imagine the negative impact that makes on attendees!

At a recent Sports Trade Show, I passed a 600-square-foot exhibit where the 25 staff members were wearing red T-shirts with the company name, marketing message, and logo. It should have been a professional, impressive sight. However, it was lunchtime and the 25 red-shirted staff were eating pizza. They were ignoring the interested attendees who, feeling like uninvited guests, passed by the booth without stopping.

Visit the Press Room

When you deliver your press kit to this room, speak to the public relations director. Even better, have a meeting prior to the show to build familiarity with your products or services. Sometimes you also can visit the press room during the show and chat spontaneously with reporters to generate extra interest.

A good public relations person can be a great asset to your efforts, yet few exhibitors take advantage of show publicity opportunities. For example, when I worked with the Sunset Home Show, we solicited press information from all of the exhibitors.

Out of 150 exhibitors, only about 20 responded to our request! Sunset developed story

---

Staff Snacks

If you have a private break room for your sales staff, have wholesome snack food available.

If you don't have a separate break room, during move-in, scope out the hall and find a quiet common area that you can recommend employees use during breaks. It's a nice touch to keep a box of "snack bags" available for your sales staff to take on breaks. Each bag might include bottled water, some nuts, and a piece of fruit. Healthful snacks keep energy levels up and let precious break time be used for relaxing instead of waiting in line to purchase food.

lines from the press information and then brought the reporters to the individual booths during the show. A photographer was on hand and, in many cases, television and radio crews. Those 20 exhibitors received free print, television, and radio publicity. Think about the 130 exhibitors that did not bother to send in materials!

Institute an End-of-Day Recap

Usually show events last more than one day. It's not too late to make some additional adjustments if you are not getting expected results. Have an "end of the day" sales meeting. Perhaps one particular staff person is having a problem. With more input, it can be solved. These meetings should be short and concise.

One exhibitor I consulted with used these meetings to reward the staff. Those people left the hall feeling energized and ready for the next day. Their sales efforts doubled during the rest of the show.

Tips for Solo Exhibitors

- Pack a lunch of "bites." If you're in the middle of eating a big deli sandwich, attendees will hesitate to interrupt you, and it looks unprofessional. Pack foods you can nibble throughout the day, one very small bite at a time—for instance peanuts, or small cubes of cheese and fruit.
- It's hard to stand all day. Outfit your booth with two high stools. That way, you can invite an interested visitor to sit with you, while still remaining at eye level with people passing by.

Walk the Show

You can learn a lot about your business by taking the time to walk through the exhibit hall and see other exhibits. Some exhibitors may be your competitors and some may be opportunities for forging new business relationships.

Many times, bigger deals can be done with other exhibitors than with attendees. Many of my clients use their participation in a trade show to find a representative for their line or service that can exhibit for them in these events. It is a cost-effective way to find a new marketing arm.

AFTER THE SHOW

Follow Up

Many leads at shows are *never* followed up. What a waste. Some big potential contacts should have your material waiting on their desks when they return. It's easy to arrange by calling your home office each day (or using a computer hook up). All leads should receive a brief note or call within a week to assess their interest. And many leads should be put in your database for regular contact.

Post-Show Analysis

As part of your participation in the show event, most reputable show management companies do provide a list of all registrations for the event. As registration equipment and software have become more sophisticated, these lists are more technical and offer complete buyer/attendee profiles. If you want to follow-up your show participation with a direct mail piece, mailing labels are usually available at an additional cost. However, these lists usually are not ready for distribution until 30 days after the show.

A thank-you letter to those people who visited your booth is an additional way to keep the contact with your customer or potential customer. You'll need to have a system of data entry for their names and addresses rather than waiting for show management to provide the list. This process should take place within five days after the show event. The memories are fresh, your notes will make sense, and your leads are hot.

Review your sales objectives and determine whether you reached your goals. Discuss the results with your sales team and get their feedback.

It Takes Repeat Contact

Research says the average sale takes seven or more contacts. Yet the average salesperson quits after two!

—Rick Crandall, *Marketing Your Services: For People Who Hate to Sell*

If you feel comfortable contacting fellow exhibitors, you might ask them about their experiences. General problems like bad weather can influence everyone in a show.

Additional items to review:
- did you meet your budget projections
- best thing about the show
- worst thing about the show
- important comments about your product/service
- should you do this market next time

IN CONCLUSION

Trade shows are a great source of marketing for a company, provided that there is a overall plan of action to take advantage of every aspect of the event. By paying attention to *before* the show, *during* the show, and *after* the show, you will have greater success.

BURST INTO ACTION

I can give you a six-word formula for success: Think things through—then follow through.

—Eddie Rickenbacker

1 Research possible shows at which to exhibit by talking to promotion companies and their exhibitors. Go to the shows whenever possible.

2 If it's your first show, decide if your booth will be reusable or a one-time effort.

3 If you exhibit at shows regularly, keep a notebook of past problems and successes for future reference.

4 Decide on an effective giveaway—one your prospects and customers will keep or remember.

5 Develop a written procedure to train exhibit staff. Decide on ways to reward your staff.

6 Develop a program of mailings/faxes/e-mail to reach customers and prospects before the show.

7 Plan your booth with both utility and memorability in mind.

8 Set up a program to follow up on show-generated leads.

ONLINE MARKETING FOR SUCCESS

Rick Crandall

Rick Crandall, PhD, is a consultant, writer, and speaker, specializing in talks and workshops on marketing, service, and sales. His philosophy is that business success today revolves around strong relationships with customers and the ensuing repeat business. He works largely with service providers and others who are uncomfortable with marketing. He has spoken to groups such as *Inc.* magazine, the American Marketing Association, Autodesk, Office Depot, the American Society for Training and Development, and many others. Dr. Crandall has presented well over 1,000 public seminars, given many keynote presentations, and worked with organizations from large law firms to the U.S. Air Force.

He is the author or editor of eight books and three tape sets on marketing including *1001 Ways to Market Your Services: Even If You Hate to Sell*, *Celebrate Customer Service*, and *Advanced Relationship Selling*.

Dr. Crandall is the recipient of an SBA Small Business Award, and is listed in various *Who's Whos*. He edits an online marketing newsletter, *Marketing Edge*. For a free subscription, send him an e-mail.

Rick Crandall, PhD; Agent: Select Press, PO Box 37, Corte Madera, CA 94976-0037; phone (415) 435-4461; fax (415) 435-4841; e-mail RPCrandall@aol.com.

Chapter 10

ONLINE MARKETING FOR SUCCESS

Rick Crandall

The Internet allows information to be distributed world-wide at basically zero cost.

—Bill Gates, Microsoft Corp.

Online marketing success stories are common currency on the Web. The one I like best is from a small local tile contractor, Bill Furner (www.pyramidtile.com).

He says there aren't many contractors online so he's been featured in the media and asked to speak. His site has won lots of awards, including a couple from realty sites that could be good referral sources. He now calls himself "Mr. Tile." Bill is self-taught on the Mac and his site is self-produced. He does a lot of upscale tile work for hot tubs, kitchens, bathrooms, and so forth. His site features appealing pictures of his jobs as well as listing resources such as books.

Surprisingly, Bill says many people have found him online. He now credits more than half of his business to his Web site. The Web appears to be a media that upscale clientele like.

Has he gotten rich beyond his wildest dreams? Absolutely not. But, if the Web can work for a local contractor, it can work for almost anyone.

The goal of this chapter is to give you an overview of online marketing and suggest some ways you can improve your efforts.

THE NEW MARKETING

The Web *is* a powerful new marketing medium. It is a great equalizer: An individual or a small company can reach the same universe of potential buyers as a large corporation.

Most people who talk about online marketing are all positive. However, the Web is also messy (searching is inefficient); it's loaded with hype, outdated information, and small-time scams.

Using the Web Effectively

Many big companies tend to approach online marketing as a medium like television—how many "eyeballs" can they reach for X dollars. More sophisticated large companies are moving toward using technology to customize their interactions with each customer.

Smaller companies sometimes go online just to keep up, or because customers expect it. Despite their lack of sophistication, small companies may achieve more online than larger companies because they are naturally—and by necessity—closer to one-to-one relationships with each customer.

Doing business online allows direct contact with customers. This may cut costs, but the greater benefit is simply allowing more people in your company to have direct, unfiltered contact with customers. Everyone in your company can now build relationships directly with customers.

> Target marketing and one-to-one marketing are not necessarily the same thing. Most target marketing programs segment your audience into groups. One-to-one marketing focuses on a segment of one.
> —Don Peppers & Martha Rogers, *The One to One Future: Building Relationships One Customer at a Time*

12 ADVANTAGES OF ONLINE MARKETING

Online marketing has many advantages that make it appealing.

1 Online marketing is **integrated marketing**. It can be your billboard, your brochure, your catalog, and your focus group. It gives you a lot of tools and flexibility in your marketing. For instance, Sierra South, a store for those who love the outdoors, replaced their print catalog with an online newsletter and special online offers. Business has never been better.

2 Online marketing can be **inexpensive**. It's also an easy entry. Simple marketing can be done with nothing but your time. And unlike other media, your costs don't necessarily go up as you provide more information.

3 Online is **faster**. You can post up-to-date information for your customers and prospects immediately. You can even send it out automatically to your list.

4 Online is **simpler**. You can save steps, both for you and your customers.

5 Online marketing is **customizable**. Customers can be presented with individualized information that speaks directly to them.

6 Online marketing gives a lot of **control to customers**. In a world of one-on-one marketing, where customers want personalized service, online leads in this direction easily and naturally.

7 Online marketing is **interactive**. Much like the personal sales process, you have a chance to get feedback from prospects and buyers.

8 Online marketing is **information-rich**. Pictures, video, sound, and text can provide more information than any other single marketing medium.

9 Online exposes you to a growing and **diverse audience**. While it does not reflect the entire country, many types of people are online. By looking for specific interest groups, you can find representatives of almost any type of person. (See Chapter 3 on niche marketing.)

10 Online marketing is **international**. You have immediate access to an international audience, whether for sales, feedback, or ideas. It's making us more and more of a "global village."

11 It's a **24-hour medium**. People can respond when they want. If you're trying to run a fast company or a 24-hour company, this is the tool that will get you there. When someone asks for information, your computer can automatically send them a response (using autoresponders), even if you're asleep at the time .

12 It allows you to **create a sense of community** with your customers. Through chat rooms, discussion groups, newsletters, and other tools, you can strenghten relationships with customers.

The Homeless Online

While the poor and uneducated tend to not be online, there are exceptions. Schools and libraries make Internet connections available widely, as well as programs that target underserved groups.

A dramatic example of individual initiative to get online occurred in Northern California. Car batteries were being stolen from road maintenance vehicles. Police found the culprit under a freeway overpass: A homeless man had stolen the batteries to power his portable computer and wireless connection to the Net!

13 WAYS TO MARKET ONLINE

Now let's look at some of the details of marketing online. There are many specific ways to market online. Here are 13 of the key ones.

1 **Your signature.** When you send a letter, you sign your name and possibly your title. For e-mail, it's traditional to have your name and an additional few lines which can be a mini ad for what you do. For instance, a signature could say, "John Smith, Construction Marketing Specialist. We help you impress architects and owners."

Your signature can also include a hotlink to your Web page. If your domain name is a great one, this can be a valuable marketing tool on its own.

When a major marketing annual publication wanted to reprint a chapter I wrote on online marketing a few years ago, they wanted to cut out this "signature" point as too "small time." They didn't understand the personal touch your signature allows you.

In one survey, the most effective method of getting people to your Web site was responses to your e-mail and signature. Even in the "netiquette" where self-promotion is sometimes frowned on, your signature line is acceptable.

2 **Give away advice.** Giving away free advice to various interest groups, chat groups, and mailing lists allows you to build relationships.

When contributing to an online discussion, learn the rules of the group first. Observe for a while, or read past "issues" or Frequently Asked Questions (FAQs).

Online Networking

About 1984, when online bulletin boards were rare, a California friend of mine became bulletin board "pen pals" with a woman in Milwaukee. They exchanged information and ideas about marketing. She eventually referred him to a friend of hers for whom he wrote a number of marketing items. (He never met either the referrer or the customer in person.)

Build Relationships

Think of e-mail as a chance to build relationships, just as you would have done by letter in the old days. Customized e-mail is the ultimate in one-to-one marketing.

E-mail combines the features of the phone and writing. People often dash off quick responses. Thus, e-mail often has a less-polished feel than might a letter that you edited and thought about.

Of course, I recommend that you edit carefully. Everything that you produce should represent you exactly the way you want it to.

3 **Links.** One of the major features of the Web is hyperlinks. You can create hot buttons where, with the click of a mouse on a word or graphic, someone can move to another area of your page or to a page anywhere in the world.

There are two ways to use these links to market yourself. One way is to link your site to other sites where people like your customers will tend to go. This makes your site more valuable, so that people will visit it more often.

Your Web page becomes the central resource. By constantly adding interesting links, people will have an incentive to come back and see what's new.

Links to you. The second way to use links is to get other sites to provide links to yours. This is the second best source of site visitors. And, of course, a link from another site is an endorsement that your site is worth visiting.

Of course, there's a danger in providing links *away* from your page. Even if they'd been intending to come back, something in your page can take

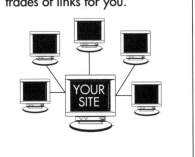

Trade Links

The Link Exchange Digest (linkexchange.com) coordinates trades of links for you.

visitors to another page, something in that page takes them to another page, and so on and so on. Pretty soon they've forgotten where they are, if they ever knew. This leads us to method #4.

4 **Encourage bookmarks.** Bookmarking is a way of recording or indexing the Web pages you've visited. Tell people on your first page to bookmark it so that they can get back easily.

You might want to mention this several places on your site, especially near material that is updated regularly, or near your best material.

5 **Web page design.** Proper design is aesthetically pleasing as well as effective.

Title Your Graphics

Graphics make your Web page look nice, but they can make Web pages load slowly. Many people turn on the "ignore graphics" option in their browser. This means no graphics are loaded and all the viewer sees is "[graphic]" in the place the graphic would be.

HINT: Construct your Web page using the "ALT=" feature. This allows you to include a one- to four-word description of the graphic. Instead of seeing "[graphic]", viewers will see "[CEO photo]" or [New Product Front View]. That way viewers can decide if it's worth down-loading a particular photo.

Getting old waiting for graphics to load

Practical Graphics Tips

In addition to the general value of "good design," there are some specific things to use.

One design issue is how you link to other Web sites. You don't want to put links on your first page. You want them to only leave your page after they have read something valuable on yours.

Another simple point is to remember to put your name, address, phone, fax, or e-mail on every page—as the computer presents them to readers. If browsers print any page, everything they need to contact you will be right there.

Remember that not everyone uses the same browser. Look at your page using different browsers to see how the presentation looks. For instance, your type is read and presented different ways by the various browsers. People on slow modems can't wait to download complex graphics, and some overseas users often can't read graphics at all. Too many pages load too slowly. Shrink graphics that slow your page down.

6 **Fresh content.** I call old pages "cobweb sites." If you aren't constantly adding new links, new articles, new research, etc., your page becomes old news.

7 **Custom pages.** By linking your Web page to a database, some programs let you create custom material for each person who visits you. For instance, NeXT Computer's Web Objects created custom Web pages as early as 1996.

8 **Directory listings.** One of the best ways (third in one survey) to be found on the Web is to get yourself listed in the many directories and indexes. Some directories, like Yahoo, try to cover most Web pages. These combine directories and search engines to help users find resources that they need. There are also services that will list you in multiple directories. (For a discussion on how to get listed, try www.searchenginewatch.com).

Reasons To Visit A Site

One direct mail consultant has a "critique of the week" on his page. He takes a mailing he receives, scans it in and tears it apart. He also has databases of marketing statistics and an index of articles people can order. By constantly updating all these, people have lots of reasons to visit his page regularly.

Key Words

This brings us to the idea of key words. Most directories and search engines look for key words (including meta tags). It's an important marketing decision what you name your Web page and what key words you use to describe it. You have to think

The Name Is the Thing

The title of your page is your first set of key words. Leave your ego behind. Maynard, Garcia, Beck may be a fine name for a law firm, but is difficult to remember. Patentlawyers.com would be a better name for a Web page.

When a poster and framing store changed their Web page name from artuframe.com [not a bad name since it gives the product], to the simpler art.com, the owners experienced an immediate 30% jump in site traffic.

in terms of the user. What are they going to be looking for? How can you help them find you?

For example, I shouldn't call my Web page "Rick Crandall's Web page." No one but my friends would search for that. Instead, I should call it the "online marketing, consulting, advertising, publicity, merchandising, retail, customer service page from Rick Crandall"!

9 Give away something. People like free things. When you can give away valuable information, postcards, graphics, and so forth, people will remember your site.

If you give away information you've developed, it is a work sample demonstrating your expertise. It can also be a free sample encouraging further purchases. For instance, several people have given away the first chapter of a book and sold the rest. Or they've given away one version of their software and sold upgrades.

The King and Queen of Spam

Spamming was made notorious by attorneys Laurence Canter and Martha Siegel. In 1994 they posted ads for their immigration services in every Usenet group they could find. People hated it and the lawyers' computer service was closed down from the "flames" and "mail bombs" they received. But they claim that they also got $100,000 of business from it. And they wrote a book.

10 Spam. Spamming is the Net's junk mail. The law is in flux on this issue. As of 1999, only a few states had laws regulating spam. And under these laws, you are allowed to solicit people once as long as you tell them it is advertising and let them tell you not to contact them again. While few people recommend spam, it is legal.

Netiquette

The online world was originally used by academics. Most material was given away. It was considered poor taste to actively promote yourself or to impose yourself on users.

In addition, much like junk faxes, users pay for their accounts and their time online. If you contact them, they have to pay for your marketing. This is an area where there will continue to be lots of conflict and evolution.

11 Your online newsletter or ezine. While technically this is a form of e-mail, it is so important that it deserves its own point. Creating a brief newsletter online is a great way to keep in touch and build relationships. It gives people a sample of your expertise and philosophy, lets them become familiar with you, reminds them of you, and makes it easy for them to respond. Having a good ezine and list can be more important than your Web site.

The trick is to develop an opt-in list where people ask for your newsletter. Start by inviting your existing customers and contacts to subscribe. Add notices of your ezine to your signature, Web site, and other ads. Then ask for referrals. You can also register with directories like:

> ### Meta Search Engines
>
> Searching online is still inefficient. A search performed using the same keywords on different search engines often produces vastly different results. Save time by using meta search engines—they simultaneously search about 20 different search engines. I use dogpile.com, but there are many others (inference. com, seeko.com, and so forth).

- ezinesearch.com
- meer.net/~john/e-zine-list/
- site-city.com/members/e-zine-master
- gizmonet.com/pufbform.htm
- ezinecenter.com
- newsletter-library.com/ven.htm
- mmgco.com/alist/

You'll find that your list builds rapidly.

12 **Affiliate programs.** Amazon.com popularized affiliate programs. In their case, you recommend books on your site, and if people want to buy them, they can click and go directly to Amazon to order. Amazon then pays you a commission (under 10%) on all sales from your site. With the success of the Amazon program, hundreds of other online affiliate programs have been created. For instance, you can earn commissions for recommending search engines, graphics sources, consultants, and almost anything else.

> The consensus is strong that relationship marketing will thrive on the Net thanks to its speed, low cost, and convenience.
>
> —*Direct* magazine

If you can pay commissions to encourage other people to sell or recommend your products or services, you may be able to set up a successful affiliate program. The best programs are really just referral sources. People put a link to you on their Web sites and recommend what you offer because they use it themselves. (Web rings linking related sites are somewhat similar.)

Unfortunately, most affiliate programs sell things that people don't need at high prices—and often the programs don't pay their commissions very reliably. There is also a sense of people "taking in each other's laundry" because many of the programs involve selling courses on how to market online. If everyone makes their money from selling instructions on how to market online, that means that everyone is just selling to newcomers who hope to sell to more newcomers. To succeed online, ultimately you'll have to sell something that isn't available everywhere else.

13 **"Cold" individual e-mail.** The definition of spam is not really fixed. It tends to mean mass, impersonal, commercial mail to people you don't know. But some people resent any contact they didn't ask for. However, I have had success sending individual notes to people I don't know.

For each note, I type in the person's name and customize the message when I can. However, I may send a similar note to many people.

For example, I may search online for Web sites of marketing consultants. I then send each an e-mail inviting them to sell my marketing books to their clients, to write a chapter in a book, or to subscribe to my free newsletter. The connection is commercial and "cold," but it potentially fits them. I might also be researching a topic and ask for information in their area.

> ### The Net Likes Attitude
>
> Because the Net is a young medium, it responds well to material with an "edge." Be a personality. Consider being quirky, funny, or "edgy."

Another firm, net-market.com, located e-mail addresses for a client in a directory maintained by the client's competitor. Thirteen percent responded to a custom e-mail. Speaker Steve Waterhouse received a 50% response from e-mailing associations about his speaking to their groups.

I've done a great deal of business online with this approach. While very few people ask me not to contact them again (less than 1%), sometimes up to 20% respond positively.

NEW MARKETING MODELS

You may notice that I haven't included Web "malls" in my list of techniques. They are a marketing dead end. They tend to be overpriced deals promoted by seminars around the country or low-level junk sites run by exploitive marketers.

You need to develop acceptable new ways to invite people to receive more information from you without offending them.

We don't have to reinvent the wheel here. In direct market-

> ### Online Mortgages
>
> Eastern Mortgage Services got 50–100 home equity loan applications a week from its Web site within months of creating it. Plus, the applications are for higher average amounts but cost Eastern only $10 to handle on-line versus $100+ the traditional way.
>
> The company approaches its offer as it would any other direct mail solicitation by making it to the point and easy to read, offering free 24-hour approval, and calling for action. To attract people, Eastern employs the "traditional" on-line marketing techniques of registering with search engines and linking with more than 200 other sites.

ing, advertising, and telemarketing, they have developed two-step marketing. This is probably the best model from traditional marketing to apply to online marketing. In fact, online will probably end up popularizing three- and four-step marketing programs.

Marketing Is About Relationships

It's all a matter of building relationships with people. For instance, let's say you have a list of e-mail addresses of people you think might be interested in your product or service. Or, even worse, you have a large list of e-mail addresses whom you know nothing about. You're tempted by the fact that it may cost you only a little time to send them all e-mail messages.

So you give in to this temptation. If you send them a commercial message, you'll be guilty of spamming. You'll get flame-mail and your service provider may even disconnect you!

Step 1: Try an Invitation

Is there another way to open the relationship? What if you sent people an invitation that said, "I wasn't sure if this was appropriate for you, but if you're interested in information on XYZ, please send me a message and I'll get you more information free. If you don't respond, I'll take you off the list and not bother you again. Thank you for your time." This would be legal spam.

Try to offer people something of real value that "fits" them. In direct mail, you might get a .5% response from a list that fit your product. My research suggests that if you spam people you don't know anything about, you might get only a .05% response. (That's 400 per 800,000 messages.) With my personalized "cold mail" (Method #13), I might get a 5% response or better—that's 100 times better than bulk spam.

Step 2: Start a Relationship

For the people who actually identify themselves as interested, the second step is to send
them the material you promised them.

You'd start off by saying, "Here's the information you asked for on XYZ." Then, in a low-key way,
you would explain any offer to them. Because
these are selected prospects, you might get a 10%
response, or more. And some of the others would
buy later.

Multi-Step Marketing

Where it would become three- or four-step
marketing is where you might not even ask for the
order the second time. You might say, "We're very
interested in getting input from new people and
seeing what they like in this area. We'll keep you
informed with free reports and other material
that become available in this area, unless you send us an e-mail message
that says you don't want to hear
anything more from us."

First they had to "opt in" to
get on your list (they had to
make a positive response). Now they have to "opt
out" to get off your list. It's like the continuity book
clubs. They'll get more information unless they
explicitly ask to be removed.

First Business

Ezine

Freebie

Contact

The Relationship Builds

You can now put these new people on your
newsletter list, press release list, or other non-
pushy communications which build the relationship. This allows them to get used to you and
builds potential trust. You might also start creating a community because you'll want to build
relationships with many people at the same time.
You'd do this with a discussion group or other tool
that allowed your audience to interact with each
other under your sponsorship.

At some point, it will become appropriate to make them an offer. For instance, your newsletter may have interesting articles and information. It may also have a note attached to it that says, "Special this month. If you'd like me to critique your internal policies manuals for the newest HR law at half price, send them to me." Or you may say, "We've just written a book on this topic and we have a free report or we have a paid report." Gradually it becomes more and more natural to offer recipients things that they could pay for.

> Success in the online marketplace isn't a sure thing . . . [but] nothing we've seen so far comes close to its potential.
> —Jay Conrad Levinson and Charles Rubin, *Guerrilla Marketing On-Line*

CONCLUSIONS

The good news is that you are still on the ground floor of a major new business medium. There's still time to be a pioneer, despite the fact that others have been experimenting with it for 25 years.

The bad news is that there is lots of worthless material online. Big companies waste money on beautifully designed pages but don't connect emotionally with their customers. And most "fancy" pages aren't designed to load fast and be user friendly. Small companies get involved in scams and "garbage." And search engines still waste lots of time and find much unrelated material.

Test Before You Spend

Success in any marketing comes from testing. And online is a great place to test. You can test different ads or offers to be used "offline." And you can test different places to market online. (See also Chapter 11.) You can track from which directories your inquiries come by using different e-mail addresses (equivalent to post office boxes in direct mail) or Web analysis tools. You can post notices to different groups using codes. You can begin to understand where actual business or viable inquiries come from.

In other words, just because online is a new and exciting medium doesn't mean old rules don't apply. Find people who need what you have to offer. Track your responses. And build relationships to do lots of business over time.

Those are the basics of good marketing—both online and offline. They will apply to any new medium.

BURST INTO ACTION
We must either find a way or make one.
—Hannibal

1 If you don't have a Web page, look for a free place to practice with one (for example, aol.com, tripod.com, or geocities. com).

2 Consider creating multiple Web pages, each focused to reach one group of customers. Then link them together.

3 Work to build your own list for an opt-in e-mail newsletter.

4 Send lots of e-mail correspondence and answer your e-mail promptly.

5 Contribute to discussion groups, or run one.

6 Get on mailing lists relevant to your interests. The I-advertising Digest (internetadvertising. org) and I-sales Digest (audettemedia.com) are good marketing ones.

7 Improve your signature line.

8 Arrange links with other related sites.

9 Improve your Web page with forms and small Java programs (applets.)

Chapter 11

ALIGN YOUR MARKET, MESSAGE, AND METHOD
The Marketing Mix System™

Ford Saeks

Ford Saeks
is one of America's top marketing mentors. His sales-
producing, profit-generating
solutions help people reach success in their new or existing business ventures by making every dollar count. For over 20 years, Mr. Saeks has been actively involved in the successful growth and operation of multiple business ventures in a variety of industries.

As president of Prime Concepts Group, Inc., Mr. Saeks is best known for positioning people and their products and services for maximum profit through his Marketing Mix System™ and innovative publicity campaigns.

Mr. Saeks is a featured television and radio guest on business and marketing issues and is the creator of "how to" products. A member of the National Speakers Association, he speaks nationally and internationally on how to improve marketing results and sales performance, Internet marketing, and electronic commerce. His clients include start-up ventures, entrepreneurs, corporations, associations, and convention groups interested in eliminating waste and increasing profits from all of their marketing and promotional efforts. Recent clients include celebrity speaker Les Brown, NationsBank, and Annex Publishing.

Ford Saeks, Prime Concepts Group, Inc., 3122 N. Tee Time Road, Wichita, KS 67205-1915; phone (800) 946-7804 or (316) 721-5575; fax (316)721-6776; e-mail ford@saeks.com; Internet www.primeconcepts.com.

Chapter 11

ALIGN YOUR MARKET, MESSAGE, AND METHOD
The Marketing Mix System™

Ford Saeks

> It is the calling of great men, not so much to preach new truths, as to rescue from oblivion those old truths which it is our wisdom to remember and our weakness to forget.
>
> —Sidney Smith

Fall 1987. I was living in a cramped, one-bedroom apartment in Wichita, Kansas. My roommates: two Italian racing bikes.

One day, as I untangled myself from the spokes of my Medici Criterion Bicycle, it came to me: a design for a product that stored bicycles in an apartment or house without taking up too much space or damaging the walls or ceiling. After some development, I decided to call this floor-to-ceiling oak bicycle rack PedaStyle®.

I had a great product. I was convinced that selling it would be the easy part.

I didn't have much money, but I did have enthusiasm. I read over 30 books by famous marketing gurus. I took careful notes. I wrote a detailed marketing plan. I was ready to sell.

I sent a sales letter and brochure to 10,000 bicycle club members. This was a bit of a stretch for me. Renting the lists, printing the brochures, and paying for the postage cost $6,500—a small fortune for a guy on a fixed salary who was overextended with monthly bills and a big car payment. But I wasn't worried. I knew I had a great product, a marketplace brimming with potential buyers, and a proven marketing strategy. My only concern was whether my tiny mailbox could hold all the orders the mailman would soon be stuffing inside it.

After four days, I checked my mailbox. I figured a couple of people would have sent their checks in by now.

Nothing.

Three . . . four . . . five weeks went by.

Not a single order.

Direct mail, I concluded, doesn't work.

Implementing Marketing: What Does It Take?

Has this ever happened to you?

You study the strategies, implement the techniques to a "T," and nothing happens.

Most marketing books are filled with hundreds—even thousands—of strategies that promise better results and higher profits with a few simple steps. So why do so many people fail to get the results they want? Is it because those strategies don't work?

Rest assured, the strategies do work. (I know. I found out the hard way.)

But it takes a special system to make the strategies produce the results they promise. The system is simple and easy to use. It can generate impressive results with very little wasted money or effort. And in a few paragraphs, I will share it with you. But first, let's return to 1987.

Nothing is ever a complete failure—it can always serve as a bad example.
—Anonymous

If at First You Don't Succeed . . .

Despite my direct mail disaster, I was still convinced that PedaStyle was the storage solution thousands of bikers had been looking for . . . and that I would get rich delivering it to them.

If direct mail wasn't the answer to my marketing dreams, I figured maybe advertising would do the trick. So I placed ads in five major cycling magazines, set up an 800 number, and offered a special low price.

The ad space cost me $7,580, and the 800 number added $50 to my tab. (I knew Aunt Belle, rest her soul, would have been pleased to know that the small inheritance she left me paid my bill at *Bicycling Magazine*.)

This time, I was convinced I had it made. My ads would reach over 350,000 bicycle enthusiasts. Even if only 2% of them responded, I'd soon be trading in my one-bedroom apartment for a down payment on a country club estate overlooking a golf course.

The issue with my ad in it came out. Only a handful of checks trickled in.

Then I took the show on the road to cycling events. I barely broke even on gas.

I tried telemarketing. Another bomb.

On the Value of Advertising

I know half of my advertising is wasted. I just don't know which half.

—John Wanamaker, department store magnate

I tried advertising in trade publications, using direct mail, and making in-person sales calls.

Sales were pathetic. I couldn't figure out what was wrong.

I had the right product. The 27 people who did buy the PedaStyle raved about it.

I had the right approach. I thought I followed the marketing strategies to the letter. I knew there was a market. Every article I read said that more and more Americans were buying (and presumably storing) bikes.

Despite my commitment to PedaStyle, my opportunity to market it was drawing to an end. I'd stripped my tiny savings accounts to pay for my campaigns. I'd sold one of my bikes to cover my living expenses. I had become so reliant on credit cards that I gave new meaning to the question "paper or plastic?" I knew I'd hit bottom when I called my landlord to ask if he took MasterCard. Next, I'd be trading in my one-bedroom apartment for a pup tent.

The Last Chance

In a last-ditch effort to save my faltering business venture, I registered to exhibit in the fall 1987 Bicycle Dealer Showcase in Long Beach, California—the premier trade event for the bicycle industry.

I was just going through the motions as I packed my old van with supplies and product samples. I wasn't sure how this attempt could succeed after all the others had failed. My friend Steve Sims agreed to come along to help. (You know you're pathetic when your friends feel so sorry for you that they'll take a week of vacation to sit behind a booth in a trade show!)

Off we headed for California.

On the first day of the show, we handed out more than a thousand brochures. That was the good news. The bad news: People loved PedaStyle, they said—but they just wanted to look around before they placed an order.

Right.

Three days later, with the trade show's close just hours away, we had only $700 in sales.

"Well," I said, "we've given it our best shot. I guess PedaStyle just isn't going to make it."

Steve and I decided to pack up early so we could get a head start on the long drive back.

I was stacking brochures in boxes when a man walked up to the booth.

> Persistence is what makes the impossible possible, the possible likely, and the likely definite.
>
> —Robert Half

"Wait a minute. Are you leaving?" he asked. "I'm the senior buyer for Performance Bicycle Catalog, and we're interested in your product."

Six minutes later, he'd placed an order for $7,500.

The next person to stop by ordered $1,600 worth of products.

We got orders for three units . . . 30 units . . . 300 units. By the end of the show, we'd sold more than $20,000 in confirmed orders. And we had projected reorders worth more than $75,000 for the next six months.

What Happened?

What I had accomplished—well, what I had accidentally stumbled upon—was getting the *right message* in front of the *right market* using the *right marketing methods.*

Over the next 12 years, using the same foundational elements, I sold millions of dollars worth of bicycle storage solutions around the world. Since then, I've used the right mix of these three key elements—message, market, and method—to duplicate that success in dozens of other distribution channels and with hundreds of other products.

I've refined that system—matching message to market and method—into the Marketing Mix System. To learn how to use it, read on.

MORE THAN JUST THE FOUR Ps

Almost every marketing book I've read, and every marketing seminar I've attended, isn't complete without mentioning the Four Ps. They were introduced over 40 years ago by Neil Borden and then modified later by many others, including me. The Four Ps tried to cover all aspects of marketing with product, price, place, and promotion.

My Marketing Mix System takes a unique approach by showing you how to determine each element and their interrelationships, then transforms them into a system to get the best results.

It's easy to assume that one part of the mix is wrong, when in fact it is another. For example, if response to a direct mail piece is poor, it could be that the answer is to change the offer, or to send it to another market, or to improve the quality of the promotional piece, instead of cutting the price. Later, we'll look at the contributions of the different elements.

The New 4 Cs of Marketing

The 4 Ps of marketing represented the seller's point of view. The 4 Cs reflect the customer's viewpoint.

- **Customer value** (vs. Product): Defining the characteristics of your product or service in terms of customers' needs.
- **Cost to the customer** (vs. Price). Determines customers' spending.
- **Convenience** (vs. Place): Looking at location from the customer's perspective.
- **Communication** (vs. Promotion): This includes advertising, personal selling, sales promotions, and other methods.

—Philip Kotler, *Kotler on Marketing*

THE 3 ELEMENTS OF THE MARKETING MIX SYSTEM

There are three elements to the Marketing Mix System:

- Your Unique Benefit Message (represented by the arrow)
- Your Specific Target Market (represented by the target)
- Your Mastery of Marketing Methods (represented by the bow you use)

First, we'll take a closer look at each concept. Second, we'll explore how to define each concept for your product or service. Third, we'll explore how you can achieve powerful marketing results by mastering the combination of these three concepts.

ELEMENT #1:
YOUR UNIQUE BENEFIT MESSAGE

A common mistake in marketing is sending no benefit message or the wrong benefit message, and then expecting the buyer to figure it out.

With the bicycle racks, I had a different benefit message for marketing to bicycle dealers than to exporters. Bicycle dealers wanted accessories where they could make at least a 50% profit margin. Exporters wanted secure territories and multiple-year deals so they could build their markets. The main benefit to consumers was saving space, but the benefit to the catalog companies was a product that created exceptional profits from the space on their page.

Different Messages

I worked with a company called Floating Swimwear® to define its messages. Floating Swimwear manufactures a one-piece swimsuit for children with a flotation device sewn inside. It helps protect children while giving adults peace of mind.

That message—that kids won't drown—appealed to parents and grandparents. But the benefit to pool and spa dealers was different. They were attracted to the company's easy payment terms (convenience), a starter kit at a special introductory price (higher margins), use as a premium for pool owners, and the fact that it was an excellent impulse item for their customers year round (increased sales).

The success strategy of defining benefits for each market applies equally to service businesses. Quantum Expositions International, Inc., produces national career and job fairs. They have one benefit message to attract attendees, another benefit message to attract event sponsorships, and a third to attract exhibitors to their expos.

> Any fool can paint a picture, but it takes a wise man to be able to market it.
> —Samuel Butler

The large size of their events and targeted sponsorship advertising attracts large numbers of attendees. The large pool of potential employees gives the exhibitors a better chance of finding quality applicants, which saves them time and money. The attendees get the opportunity to learn about companies with job openings, and get face-to-face interviews with prospective employers, which gives them an increased advantage over applicants who merely send in their resumes. The event sponsors, usually newspapers, radio, and television stations, benefit by receiving a percentage of the exhibitors' payments from booth spaces.

With my consulting and training business, the unique benefit message I promote is that I help businesses make the most of every marketing dollar through a system that gives them a competitive edge and increased profits—guaranteed!

How can I afford to offer a money-back guarantee? Because most businesses are only using one or two marketing strategies and get the majority of their sales from only one target market. First, I evaluate their current results. Then the Marketing Mix System finds new combinations based on their resources that complement what they are already doing. This adds more value to more people, thus increasing sales and profits. The results come from new channels of distribution, increased effectiveness of their marketing efforts, higher repeat sales, and higher profit per order.

You too can achieve even greater success by mastering these three key concepts and designing the combinations for your particular business.

Features versus Benefits

Most companies focus on features and forget the benefits. You can't leave out the benefits and expect the buyer to figure them out.

This is important, because *benefits are the only reason* people pay attention to what you're selling. People want what's in it for them—what your solution will do for them.

F-A-B...ulous Benefits

Another way to summarize the features versus benefits distinction is FAB, or fabulous. You want what you do to be fabulous. Your

Features give you . . .
Advantages that provide . . .
Benefits for your customers.

Therefore, your offering is fabulous for customers.

—Rick Crandall, *Marketing Your Services: For People Who Hate to Sell*

Features are important—they add credibility—but are only valid once the buyer is aware of the benefits to them.

Creating Your Unique Benefit Message

Why should I do business with you instead of someone else? What benefits do you offer that make you unique for your target market?

The answer to those questions is your message. You might also have heard your message referred to as your "unique selling proposition" (USP), a term coined by Rosser Rieves in the 1950s. To create your message, identify your features and benefits. (See also Chapter 1.)

Gather your company's promotional materials, ads, Web site pages, and Yellow Pages listings. Next, take a note pad and draw a line down the middle of the page. Label one column "Features" and the other column "Benefits." Then search each item for the features and benefits offered and record them in the appropriate column.

Be careful not to confuse features with benefits. If it's about you, your product, your service, or your company, then it's a feature. (See the box for examples.)

Repeat the process for each product or service group on a separate piece of paper. By now, you should have a long list of benefits and features. Don't be concerned if some of your benefits don't appeal to all of your audiences. What's important at

---

Examples of Features and Benefits

- "Open 24 hours" is a feature; the benefit is convenience.
- "Low Price" is a feature; the benefit is saving money.
- "In business since 1985" is a feature; the benefit is the feeling of confidence it provides the buyer.
- "Quick delivery" is a feature; the benefit is saving time.
- "Handcrafted from solid Appalachian Oak" is a feature; the benefit is that it's attractive.
- Offering a "100% money-back guarantee" is a feature; the benefit is that there is no risk.
- "Available in five colors" is a feature; the benefit is being able to match your decor or taste.
- "Radio dispatched" is a feature; fast response is the benefit.
- "Pentium II 300MHZ" is a feature; higher performance and speed are the benefits.
- "Windows 98" is a feature; the benefit is a visually driven operating system that's easy to learn.

this stage is that you have a list of why people should buy your products and services.

What are the top five benefits from your products or services? Are those benefits clearly stated on your promotional materials through headlines, subheads, and body copy? Are they aimed at your target markets? If not, how are your customers supposed to figure out why they should do business with you? The key is to craft a message that communicates the benefit of each product and service you sell to each segment of your buying audience.

Now that you're armed with your unique benefit messages, focus them at the best targets (Element #2) and send them using the most effective methods (Element #3).

ELEMENT # 2:
YOUR SPECIFIC TARGET MARKETS

In today's highly competitive, high tech marketplace knowing as much as possible about your specific buyers and their habits is critical to achieving maximum results. Results can be measured many ways—for example, in total responses or total percentage of profit. I always aim to add the most value that maximizes the return on investment. Therefore, I want to sell to target markets that have the largest volume potential where I can still make a profit.

When I was selling PedaStyle, for example, my most profitable sale was direct to the consumer, although 90% of the revenues came from the specialty mail-order companies, like The Sharper Image, Frontgate, Herrington, and Williams Sonoma's *Hold Everything* catalogs. That meant we had to carefully craft specific benefit messages for each target market while making sure we didn't create conflict between the different distribution channels.

For example, the bicycle shops didn't want us to sell to the catalog companies because customers could use their store to view the product, and then order from the catalog company to save money. Likewise, the catalog companies didn't want us selling to the mass merchants because of the reduced retail price points. Understanding, this issue goes way beyond the normal issues of just demographics and into the psychology of the target market.

Market Subtleties

> From Montreal to Munich to Melbourne, the world is too large and filled with too many diverse people and firms for any single marketing strategy to satisfy everyone.
>
> —David L. Katz

Who you think your market is may not necessarily be the most profitable market or the only market you should pursue. For instance, I knew the many benefits of my bicycle racks, and thought that one large target market would be bicycle racers. They fit my idea of a target market.

Most bicycle racers owned more than one bike, each bike was valued at over $500 each, so racers should want the benefit of saving space and protecting their investment in bicycles. But even though they seemed like a target market, racers were more interested in spending their money on new components and traveling to bicycle races than on storing their bicycles.

When I first met with the folks at Floating Swimwear, they were operating out of their basement and selling their product at consumer boat shows. Makes sense, doesn't it? People who own boats probably have children and are definitely around water. The company was in their eighth year of business with annual revenues that hadn't exceeded $30,000. This was an absolute shame because the product had so much unrealized potential.

It was only after applying the Marketing Mix System that a much larger target market was developed. It changed their target market from consumer direct to selling wholesale to pool and spa dealers. Floating Swimwear transformed itself into a market leader with sales over $750,000 in just a few years.

Better Targeting and Better Results

Quantum Expositions International started by producing career fairs in the Midwest, with their only source of income from selling exhibit space at their expos. After looking closely at their target markets, they decided to market to major television and newspapers for sponsorships. This single move in target marketing tripled their revenues for the following two events.

Celebrity speaker and national bestselling author Les Brown gives motivational talks to corporations, associations, and conventions. His annual revenues are measured in millions. While he gets several bookings from corporate audiences each year, the bulk of speaking and product sales come from events for entrepreneurs and network marketers. This fits as his themes are "Live Your Dreams" and "It's Possible." By focusing marketing efforts on those target markets, and developing new products designed just for them, we were able to dramatically increase his income and he continues to be in high demand.

The point is to evaluate who you are actually targeting with

How to Define Your Target Markets

Ask yourself these questions:

1. What are the top three largest markets of people which can benefit most from the value of my products or services?

2. What criteria are we using to categorize the different target markets?

3. Do they have the means and authority to make purchases?

4. What is the growth potential of the top three markets? Are they growing or shrinking in size of market?

5. Who are we aiming our benefit message towards right now?

6. What characteristics are being used to distinguish our target markets?

7. What markets are my competitors aiming at?

8. What are we using to track customer data?

9. Do we have a database of prospects and customers?

10. How often do we send a benefit message to them?

11. What demographic data have we collected?

12. What do we know about their reasons for buying from us?

your marketing and promotional efforts. What evidence have you gathered that proves you should continue to pursue or go after a specific target market?

Your answers to the questions in the box on the previous page will help you recognize your specific target markets. Each product and service is unique. It's critical that you gather and track information about your customers and the effectiveness of your marketing efforts.

Did you notice any new target markets in your list? What can you do to improve the gathering of data about your customers?

By now you should have your list of unique benefit messages, and know who you want to reach with them. The next element explores the different options available to deliver your message to the target to score a bull's-eye.

ELEMENT # 3
YOUR MASTERY OF MARKETING METHODS

Most people know what the basic marketing methods are, but are not sure how to use them to their best advantage. The purposes of this section are to make you aware of the major categories of marketing methods, and show that these methods must be combined properly with your unique benefit message and target market.

The marketing methods are divided into two subcategories:

- Cash (methods that you have to pay for, like advertising)
- No cash (methods that you get for free or almost free, like publicity)

Methods that Cost You Money

Methods that cost you money consist mainly of advertising and selling mediums where you pay to have your benefit message sent to a particular audience. You can use print, radio, television, Internet, trade shows, telemarketing, or in-person sales calls. The specifics vary greatly depending upon your business.

Avoid image advertising and stick with direct response methods. Businesses often fall prey to the media advertising salesperson who talks in terms of image advertising. But, there is no way to accurately measure whether or not this type of advertising is successful. When I ask clients if their current image advertising is working they say, "We're not sure but we are getting our name out and getting exposure." Do you know what you get from exposure? A cold!

Direct response advertising methods are measurable. It is easy to know immediately if they are working. An example of direct response advertising for the bicycle racks was an advertisement in bicycle magazines offering "Buy two and get one free with no shipping expenses through the end of the month by calling 800-555-5555 x 230." (We didn't have an extension 230; it was just a device to let us know which advertisement triggered the response.)

> ### Lead with Benefits
>
> If you are going to spend your resources on advertising, make sure you lead with benefits, substantiate your claim with features, have a specific offer, and include an action step that tells the prospect what to do (call, write, and so forth). Support it with a system for tracking the responses.

Floating Swimwear advertised a "new dealer starter kit" for $548 in their industry trade magazines using a special toll-free number. They also exhibited at the National Pool & Spa shows across the country and generated more orders at one three-day show than in the entire previous year.

Dangerous assumptions. Making assumptions about your markets can be costly, as the following two examples show.

One of Floating Swimwear's distributors decided to run display ads in *USA Today*. Convinced that the large readership would yield hundreds of orders from just a few ads, they spent $18,000 on advertising. They sold 36 swimsuits! The benefit message was right, but the target market and the marketing method did not fit the product.

Another dealer decided to create a television commercial. His deciding factor was that he was getting such a great deal on the "air time," he couldn't pass it up. He did his initial research and selected markets that had large numbers of homes with pools—hardly a proper marketing test. They invested over $50,000 and sold fewer than 75 units! The commercial was good. The problem was that not many parents of small children are up watching television at 3:00 a.m. when advertising rates are low.

In these two cases, it was not the method that failed, but the combination and the faulty implementation of the method.

Test, test, test. For my consulting and speaking services, I send direct response sales letters to targeted lists and offer solutions to increase sales, productivity, and profits. The solutions are supported by free "value added" special reports and audiocassettes filled with marketing techniques that prospects can implement immediately to achieve better results. For each specific market, I craft a new unique benefit message and track the results. I start with small mailings and test different offers, pricing, and lists. Once I find a combination with a good response, I mail on a larger scale.

For the bicycle racks, we tested many different paid methods of marketing. Each target market and channel of distribution had its own combination of these concepts that made it successful. We attracted most of our dealers, catalog retailers, and exporters from industry trade shows. But the awareness of our products came from the thousands of dollars worth of free publicity we received year after year.

List the paid forms of marketing methods that you are currently using on a piece of paper. Are you tracking their effectiveness with responses?

Why Spend Money When You Can Get It for Free?

When was the last time you sent out a media release about your products or services? Free publicity is often overlooked and underutilized. It's amazing that people don't take advantage of this category of marketing methods more often.

For my line of bicycle racks, I sent out hundreds of media releases each quarter. When editors had the room in their magazines, they would run my releases. It created credibility through third-party validation. Each year, we would hear, "We see your ads everywhere; how can you afford to run so much advertising?" We couldn't afford it—it was mostly the free media releases. Sending media and press releases continues to be one of our best methods of marketing for our clients.

Tip #1: When you prepare the release, use the term "Media Release" for television and radio and "Press Release" for print media. Getting those terms mixed

7 Reasons Why You Need Free Publicity

1. Establishes credibility about you and your products or services.
2. Enhances customer retention.
3. Makes it easier to enter new markets.
4. Creates a competitive advantage.
5. Helps to position your products or services in your target markets.
6. Helps you sell more.
7. The price is right. It's practically free!

Three Media/Press Releases That I Will Create Are:	
Benefit Message	Publication or Station
1.	1.
2.	2.
3.	3.

Basic Anatomy of a Media/ Press Release

A media-press release is nothing more than a sales letter without a salutation or a signature.

1 Start with a unique benefit message in the form of a headline and subhead that focuses on the target market.

2 In the first paragraph, mention your name and the compelling messages and benefits that you offer. You might want to use bullet points for easy reading. In most cases, it's critical to tie your benefits to hot or current topics.

3 The next couple of paragraphs should state why you or your company are unique and why you have credibility to offer such solutions.

4 The closing paragraph is the action step that you want your readers, listeners, or viewers to do (for example, call for a free report, come to our event, etc.).

up is a red flag to the editors and producers, and your release may end up in the trash before they even look at it.

Tip #2: Many publications struggle each month to fill advertising space and welcome articles and product releases that add value for their audiences.

Send out press releases each month to multiple media. To find appropriate media outlets for your industry, profession, or topics, go to the library and check out the reference section for directories of publications. One great resource is the *Standard Rate & Data Service* (SRDS) directory.

MASTERING THE METHODS

There are several great resources that go into step-by-step detail on how to use different marketing methods. Many of them are covered in others chapters in this book. Think of marketing methods as the devices used to send your unique benefit messages to your specific target markets. Each concept by itself is important, but only when they are used together in the right combinations do they become powerful. Your results increase exponentially when you combine multiple marketing methods tailored to each target market.

Putting It All Together: Test

I've sat in on several focus groups and meetings where people sat around and speculated on which market would be better than another, and on what method they should use. Guessers occasionally get lucky, but usually their efforts miss their marks. The key to success is testing.

I recently worked with a company to write a direct marketing sales letter. They were clear on their market and the benefits, but not sure about the best approach.

I wrote two different headlines and split the initial test mailing in half. Each half received a different headline with a unique extension after the phone number so we could track the responses. One headline outpulled the other by 2 to 1! If we hadn't tested headlines, and only had used what turned out to be the weaker headline, we might have concluded that mailings weren't worthwhile.

Of course, you should gather market research and plan a marketing strategy, but you'll never really know what's working for you without testing. Test, test, and then—that's right—test again.

Test by sending your *unique benefit messages* to different *specific target markets* and tracking the responses from each *marketing method*. Start small and repeat the tests until you get the response rate that is acceptable to you.

Marketing is a science *and* an art. The science part is to test everything—your headlines, the copy, the colors, the markets, your benefit messages, price points—and then to keep track of the results. The art is in choos-

Marketing Mix System "Keepers"

- Even if you have the best product idea in the world, you still have to get it in front of the right decision makers.
- It's your application of the strategy that counts, not the marketing strategy itself.
- You must clearly understand who your buyers are and know as much about them as possible.
- Who you think your market is may not actually be the people to whom you are selling.
- Select the right benefits and target them for each buying market.
- Start with a small test. Test, and then test again. Then increase your efforts.

ing what to test. Once you find a winning combination, repeat it and expand it.

SUMMARY

There are four basic ways to increase your profits:

- increase your number of customers
- increase the average sale
- increase the number of repeat sales
- reduce your operational and manufacturing expenses.

The four most important questions you'll ever ask are:

1. What does it cost me to get a lead in each target market?

- You can calculate this by dividing your marketing expenses by the number of leads you get. If you spend $5,000 on a mailing to a specific target market and you get 100 leads, then the cost of attracting each lead was $50.

2. What percentage of leads is converted to customers?

- In the above example, if you get 100 leads and 20 turn into sales, your percentage is 20%.

3. What is my average up-front profit?

- This is an average of how much profit you gained per order. Simply take your selling price and subtract your cost of goods sold (COGS). Some organizations like to include promotional expenses in the COGS formula, but don't include your operating expenses in this scenario.

4. What is the long-term residual value of each customer in my specific target markets?

- Track the purchases of each customer over time in terms of repeat sales dollars and referrals.

These questions are the foundation for success or failure in your business. Armed with the answers to these questions, you can design the right combinations to dramatically improve your marketing results.

BURST INTO ACTION

A terrible thing happens without constant marketing . . . Nothing!

—P.T. Barnum

Follow these six steps to success with the Marketing Mix System:

1 Complete the features and benefits exercise and design your unique benefit messages for each valuable solution that you offer.

2 Select the top three or four markets that you feel have the most potential and gather as much information about them as possible.

3 Study the different paid marketing methods. List the ones that you feel would be the most cost-effective to reach your target market.

4 Send out press releases with benefits aimed at each specific audience.

5 Apply the Marketing Mix System elements and implement a test.

6 Evaluate your results, modify only one element at a time, and test again until you find the best combinations.

INDEX